Ripley's Believe It or Not!®

TOTALLY BIZARRE!

TOTALLY BIZARRE!

PUBLISHING

a Jim Pattison Company

Developed and produced by Miles Kelly Publishing Ltd in association with Ripley Publishing

Executive Vice President Norm Deska
Vice President, Archives and Exhibits Edward Meyer
Archives Executive Assistant Viviana Ray
Researcher Lucas Stram

Publishing Director Anne Marshall

Managing Editor Rebecca Miles
Project Manager Gemma Simmons
Text Sheri Bell-Rehwoldt, Luke Seaber, Geoff Tibballs, Tracey Turner
Editorial Assistant Charlotte Marshall
Copy Editor Catriona O'Shaughnessy
Proofreader Judy Barratt

Project Design Rocket Design
Cover Design Samantha South
Reprographics Stephan Davis, Ian Paulyn
Production Manager Liz Brunwin

Sales and Marketing Morty Mint

ISBN: 978-1-893951-30-3

10 9 8 7 6 5 4 3 2 1

Library of Congress Cataloging-in-Publication Data
Bell-Rehwoldt, Sheri.
  Ripley's believe it or not! : totally bizarre / text, Sheri Bell-Rehwoldt ... [et al.].
      p. cm.
  Includes index.
  ISBN 978-1-893951-30-3
1. Curiosities and wonders. I. Title. II. Title:
    Totally bizarre.
AG243.B419 2007
031.02--dc20
                                    2007045957
Printed in China

PUBLISHER'S NOTE
While every effort has been made to verify the accuracy of the entries in this book, the Publishers cannot be held responsible for any errors contained in the work. They would be glad to receive any information from readers.

WARNING
Some of the stunts and activities in this book are undertaken by experts and should not be attempted by anyone without adequate training and supervision.

Contents

Ripley's World

In December 1918, while working as a sports columnist for the New York Globe, Robert Ripley created his first collection of odd facts and feats.

The cartoons, based on unusual athletic achievements, were submitted under the heading "Champs and Chumps," but his editor wanted a title that would describe the incredible nature of the content. So, after much deliberation, the title was changed to "Believe It or Not!" The cartoon was an instant success and the phrase "believe it or not" soon entered everyday speech.

Ripley's passion was travel and by 1940 he had visited no fewer than 201 countries. Wherever he went, he searched out the bizarre for inclusion in his syndicated newspaper cartoons, which had blossomed to reach worldwide distribution, being translated into 17 different languages and boasting a readership of 80 million people. During one trip he crossed two continents and covered over 24,000 mi (39,000 km) "from New York to Cairo and back" to satisfy his appetite for the weird.

Ripley, on board a ship returning from South Africa in 1933, displays a set of impressive water-buffalo horns that he collected on his trip.

"Believe It or Not" Ripley

THE OFFENDING HAND

Ripley used a print of this as a postcard, to notify contributors that their submission was going to be included in one of his cartoons.

Zaro Agha, at the age of 153, was featured as the world's oldest groom in Ripley's first Believe It or Not! book. Ripley met Agha in 1927 in Turkey where he demonstrated his remarkable fitness.

Ripley sold an astonishing number of Believe It or Not! books throughout the 1920s, 1930s, and 1940s.

Ripley's Legacy Lives On

Although he died in 1949 (after collapsing on the set of his weekly television show), his "Believe It or Not!" cartoons are still produced on a daily basis—just as they have been every day since 1918—making Ripley's the longest-running syndicated cartoon in the world.

Intrepid researchers follow in Robert Ripley's footsteps, continually scouring the world and enabling Ripley's to remain the undisputed king of the strange and unbelievable. With a huge computer database of incredible facts, people, and events, a massive photographic archive, and a warehouse stuffed with unique exhibits, Ripley's is able to present a celebration of the amazing diversity of our world, without ever passing

judgment. From the outset, Robert Ripley encouraged his dedicated readers to submit material and photographs—a tradition that exists to this day. His weekly mailbag sometimes exceeded 170,000 letters! The one man who started it all was once commemorated by a memorial in his hometown church of Santa Rosa, California. The entire church was made from a single giant redwood tree.

Ripley's famous "live on location" broadcasts were always out of the ordinary. He is seen here helping to milk a rattlesnake of its venom in Ocala, Florida, in 1936.

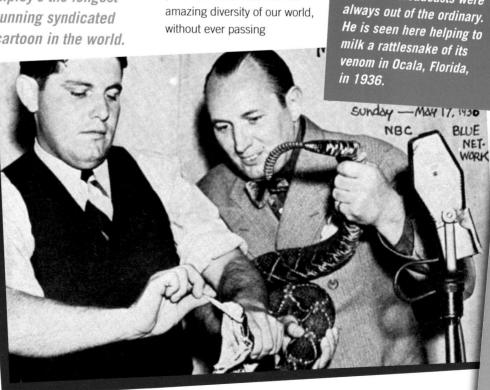

Sunday — May 17, 1930
NBC   BLUE NETWORK

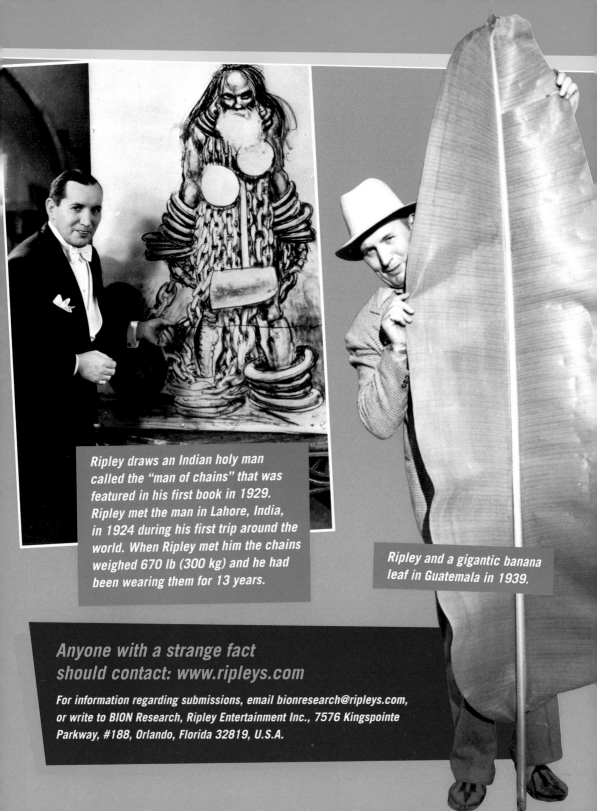

Ripley draws an Indian holy man called the "man of chains" that was featured in his first book in 1929. Ripley met the man in Lahore, India, in 1924 during his first trip around the world. When Ripley met him the chains weighed 670 lb (300 kg) and he had been wearing them for 13 years.

Ripley and a gigantic banana leaf in Guatemala in 1939.

Anyone with a strange fact should contact: www.ripleys.com

For information regarding submissions, email bionresearch@ripleys.com, or write to BION Research, Ripley Entertainment Inc., 7576 Kingspointe Parkway, #188, Orlando, Florida 32819, U.S.A.

Ripley in New York

From the first odditorium, built in Chicago in 1933, Ripley's collection is now showcased in 27 museums spread across nine countries.

On June 21, 2007, Ripley's opened its fourth New York "Odditorium" on 42nd Street, 68 years after the original New York museum opened.

During the 1930s, Ripley built six "temporary" Believe It or Not! odditoriums. The structures were part of the midway (sideshows) at World's Fair Expositions. To Ripley's dismay and anger, he lost the contract to build one at the 1939 New York World's Fair—the contract went to his main rival John Hix, "Strange As it Seems." As a result, Ripley built a museum at the corner of 48th Street and Broadway.

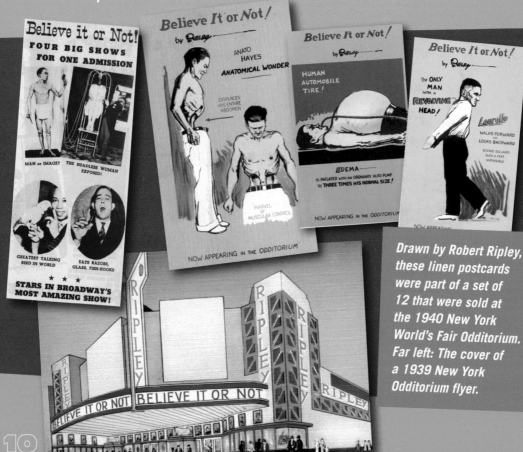

Believe it or Not!

FOUR BIG SHOWS FOR ONE ADMISSION

MAN or IMAGE?   THE HEADLESS WOMAN EXPOSED!

GREATEST TALKING BIRD IN WORLD   EATS RAZORS, GLASS, FISH-HOOKS

★ ★ ★
STARS IN BROADWAY'S MOST AMAZING SHOW!

Believe It or Not!
by Ripley

ANATO HAYES
ANATOMICAL WONDER

DISPLACES HIS ENTIRE ABDOMEN

MARVEL OF MUSCULAR CONTROL

NOW APPEARING IN THE ODDITORIUM

Believe It or Not!
by Ripley

HUMAN AUTOMOBILE TIRE !

EDEMA IS INFLATED WITH AN ORDINARY AUTO PUMP TO THREE TIMES HIS NORMAL SIZE !

NOW APPEARING IN THE ODDITORIUM

Believe It or Not!
by Ripley

The ONLY MAN WITH A REVOLVING HEAD !

Leacello
WALKS FORWARD AND LOOKS BACKWARD

SCIENCE DECLARES SUCH A FEAT IMPOSSIBLE

Drawn by Robert Ripley, these linen postcards were part of a set of 12 that were sold at the 1940 New York World's Fair Odditorium. Far left: The cover of a 1939 New York Odditorium flyer.

Lit up in lights—the New York Ripley museum in Times Square.

Exhibits on display inside the new museum.

The museum opened on July 12, 1939, and featured artifacts Ripley had collected while traveling around the world, as well as a continuous theater presentation of live human oddities and stunt performers.

The Ripley museum was a great success and, more importantly, Hix's show at the fair wasn't. In 1940, Ripley was asked to move his show to the Fair site. To begin with, he kept both his New York odditoriums open, but this proved difficult, so he closed the Broadway show, and at the end of 1940 the World's Fair site also closed.

Ripley reopened his New York museum on Broadway at 46th Street in 1957—it was open for 15 years, closing in 1972. The museum went through several changes, at one time displaying almost entirely Oriental art, then changing to medieval torture items, and toward the end it changed its name to the "Ripley Wax Museum." Perhaps the most memorable thing about this show was that for several years the doorman, who dressed in a Middle-Eastern genie costume, was the world's tallest man measuring 8 ft 4 in (2.5 m).

Today's New York museum is the largest Ripley museum in the world and twice the size of most. It features more than 500 displays, including items from Robert Ripley's personal collection as well as newer items obtained over the years by the company that he left behind.

The museum also features several videos of the hit Ripley's TV show, and the world's largest display of genuine Ecuadorian Jivaro human shrunken heads.

Was That A Good Idea?

Bent Out of Shape

Donald Hambly can bend iron bars using only his neck!

The steel rods could puncture Donald's throat at any time during the act, but his skill and concentration ensure his safety.

Putting great faith in the Shaolin monk meditation he practices, Donald positions the bars against his throat and gradually moves forward, bending them as he goes.

To begin with, the bars are moved into place and Donald starts to push!

It starts to give as he applies pressure against the bars.

He stays tense and alert as the bars gradually bend in the middle.

One final push toward the end, and he's almost there!

Pup, Pup, and Away

Buddy the Labrador and his owner, Bill Kimball of San Diego, California, have been hang-gliding together for more than eight years. Buddy's first flight took place when he was a six-month-old pup. Since then, he has joined Bill on more than 75 flights.

The car has text painted on it reading: "JUST COMPLETED AFTER BEING OVER HAULED BY HENRY H. BAYERL BLINDFOLDED"

Out of Sight

Henry Bayerl of Portsmouth, Ohio, managed to completely overhaul a car while wearing a blindfold.

Cutting Corners

Sami Sure, a construction worker in Beirut, Lebanon, couldn't afford to pay his barber 65 cents for a shave, so he gave him half of his lottery ticket instead. The ticket won and the barber scooped $133,000.

Breach of the Peace

A concert composed by Luciano Berio was once held to promote world peace. Halfway through the concert, a cannon was fired that injured several people in the audience and then caused a riot to break out.

Big Shot

One time when General George Custer was hunting buffalo, he accidentally shot his own horse!

From a Scream to a Whisper

Ever wanted to scream out loud during a stressful situation? Well now you can with an invention that allows the "stressee" to shout into a small ball that is filled with special foam. The foam muffles the noise, making it seem like a whisper.

Bullet-proof Pizza

When Cole Woolner of Michigan was delivering two deep-dish pizzas, his life was saved—by the pizzas! A bullet hit the pies and missed him.

Gone Fishing

The "Aquariass" which attaches to a working toilet, is a quirky cistern fitted with a real aquarium. But don't worry, the fish aren't actually flushed away!

Eyes Like a Hawk

A birdwatcher used a CB radio to bring twitchers flocking to a field on the Isles of Scilly, off the southwest coast of England, to see a nighthawk, a rare visitor from America. Only when telescopes and binoculars were trained on it did it become apparent that the "rare bird" was in fact a cowpat!

Name Dropping

Cleston Jenkins of Kentucky had the first names of each of his seven ex-wives tattooed on his arm.

rs
e Brazilian
ed bank-notes

Give and Take

In 1795, Boston millionaire James Swan paid off the American national debt to France, a total of $2,024,900, from his own pocket! However, unfortunately, he spent the last 22 years of his life in jail, as the French government sent him to Saint Pelagie Prison for debtors.

Mississippi Blues

Instead of taking his vehicle to a proper car wash, a man from Hannibal, Missouri, decided to save money by cleaning it in the nearby Mississippi River. He carefully backed it into a foot of water, but when he got out to start washing it, the car floated away. The police later recovered it some way downstream.

Blowing Hot and Cold

A British man got more than he bargained for when his lips became stuck to the lock on his car door while he was blowing on it in order to defrost it!

Musical Chairs

Some people sing in the shower, some even sing on the toilet, but fancy having a toilet sing to you! This singing loo, by Swiss inventors Reto Marogg and Roger Weisskopf, was presented at the annual exhibition of inventions in Geneva.

Snake Bite

Jack Bibby actually put live rattlesnakes in his mouth.

Clean and Sober

After stealing cash from a Colorado Springs corner store, an armed robber demanded a bottle of whiskey from the shelf. The clerk refused to serve him because he didn't believe he was 21. To prove he was, the robber obligingly showed the clerk his driver's licence—bearing his full name and address.

Talk is Cheap

Unable to find a summer job, teenager Trevor Dame tried to earn money by giving out advice on a street corner in his hometown of Kelowna, British Columbia. Aware that his advice might not be of the highest quality, he wore a sign around his neck saying, "Mediocre advice—25 cents."

Wake-up Call

In 1907, a patent was filed for an alarm clock that sprays water onto the face of a sleeping person.

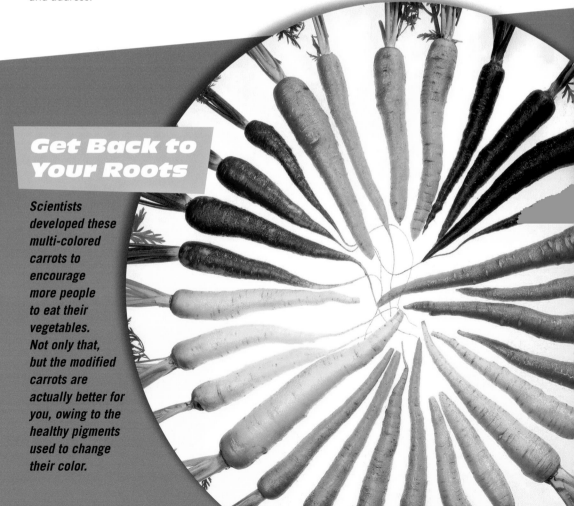

Get Back to Your Roots

Scientists developed these multi-colored carrots to encourage more people to eat their vegetables. Not only that, but the modified carrots are actually better for you, owing to the healthy pigments used to change their color.

Inflated Innovation!

Now here's an invention you can drink to— the first inflatable pub!

The traveling tavern can hold up to 30 visitors at a time. English designer Andi Francis worked on the idea for nine months after deciding to create a drinks marquee with a bit more flare than a beer tent.

The interior of the blow-up bar has everything you might expect in the real thing. It comes complete with fireplace (which is, of course, purely decorative), a stuffed fish mounted on one wall, mock Tudor beams, and lattice windows.

The Finger of Suspicion

When arrested in 2003, a Nigerian man chewed off his own fingertips so that his prints couldn't be taken. He soaked his fingers in the jail toilet, then chewed away the softened skin.

Early Warning System

A man went into a McDonald's in Sydney, Australia, at 8.50 a.m. one day in 2000, produced a gun, and demanded cash. The girl serving said she couldn't open the till without a food order. So the robber ordered a Big Mac, but was told that they weren't available until 10.30 because only the breakfast menu was being offered at that time. Frustrated, the gunman gave up and walked out.

An Unscheduled Flight

An airport baggage-handler made an unscheduled flight from Dallas to Mexico in 2001 after accidentally locking himself in the plane's cargo hold. Crew members reported that they could hear a knocking sound at Dallas, but weren't able to trace it.

Pulling a Fast One

A 41-year-old man from Barrie, Canada, who pretended to be a traffic policeman was sentenced to six months in jail after he pulled over a real detective for speeding.

Finger Stuck

An Illinois man who got his finger stuck in a pay-phone for three hours was taken to the hospital with the phone still attached to his hand. Passers-by, fire crews, and a workman from the phone company all failed to free him, until, eventually, paramedics cut the phone from its base and took the man—and the phone—to the hospital.

Playing with Fire

Bestselling children's novelist, G.P. Taylor, accidentally burned original manuscripts for three of his bestselling novels: Shadowmancer, Wormwood, and Tersias. While clearing out his house in preparation for moving, Taylor mistook the manuscripts for old paperwork and burned them to cinders.

Pot Shot

J.G. Levack, an exhibition shooter from Connecticut, tossed a golf ball in the air and hit it with a rifle bullet. He did this with such accuracy that it landed on a green with 150 yd (137 m) distance.

By the Skin of his Teeth

Sri Lankan farmer Gamini Wasantha Kumara displays extraordinary pulling power. Gamini is seen here biting down on a harness in preparation for his train-pulling challenge at Colombo's main railway station in 2001.

A Lingering Kiss

A pair of teenagers kissing in their car at traffic lights in Rio de Janeiro, Brazil, held up traffic for two-and-a-half hours when their dental braces became entwined.

By Hook or by Crook

A 36-year-old man who robbed an Ontario discount store was quickly arrested, mainly because he made no attempt to disguise the metal hook that he used in place of a hand.

Natural Wastage

Government officials in Sydney, Nova Scotia, spent $410,000 erecting a fence topped with barbed wire around a toxic-waste site in 2001. As they fixed it so that the barbed wire faced inward, the fence allowed easy access to the hazardous site but then trapped trespassers inside!

In Training

Gamini Wasantha Kumara pulled the 40-ton railway carriage a total of more than 80 ft (25 m) in Colombo, Sri Lanka, using only the harness gripped between his teeth!

Chin Up

Robert Dotzauer from Los Angeles could balance three lawnmowers on his chin at the same time.

The Price You Pay

A St. Louis janitor got his finger stuck in a pay-phone change slot and spent three hours trying to dislodge it while passers-by laughed at his predicament. He finally thought to use his free hand to call 911.

Sweet Dreams

A Japanese toy firm claims to have devised a gadget that can help people to control their dreams. They say the Dream Workshop can be programmed before bedtime to help sleepers choose who or what they want to dream about.

Giving Up the Ghost

In 2004, the ghost of Indiana man Collin Proctor, in the form of his walking-cane, was sold on auction website eBay for $65,100. Mary Anderson of Hobart, Indiana, put her father's ghost up for sale to help her young son to cope with his grandfather's death. She asked the buyer to write to the boy acknowledging receipt of the ghost. Sadly, the sale came back to haunt her as the resultant publicity gave her insomnia.

Tunnel Vision

The driver of this car was caught in a sticky situation after mistaking the entrance to the subway for a ramp into a parking garage in Paris, France. Firemen were called in to rescue the car from slipping further down into the underground tunnels.

Sleeping Partner

In 2002, a Romanian pensioner ran up a bill of £950 ($1,900)—the equivalent of the average annual salary in Romania—after falling asleep while on a phone chat line.

Opening Shelved

In Gloucestershire, England, a council had to inform residents that a new £2-million ($4-million) library would not be opening on schedule in 2003 because the council had forgotten to order any books or shelves!

Under the Knife

A man from Chino Valley, Arizona, who had been playing with a knife by tossing it into the air, was taken to hospital with a 12-in (30-cm) steak knife firmly embedded in the back of his head.

The Milk of Human Kindness

A woman in Nanjin, China, ordered 3,000 barrels of milk over a three-month period in the name of a local university as she feared that her boyfriend, a dairy company sales manager, would be recalled to their head office because of poor milk sales.

Injury Time

There were so many injuries during 2004's Women's National Festival of Rugby in Staffordshire, England, that emergency services termed it "a major incident." Ten ambulances and a helicopter dealt with ruptured muscles, broken bones, and even a dislocated hip.

Log Jam

Kenneth Lambert of New Hampshire crossed the log-jammed Androscoggin River on snow skis.

Taking the Plunge

Diving 29 ft (9 m) into water may not sound too challenging, but it certainly is when the water is only 12 in (30 cm) deep!

Louisiana-born diver Danny Higginbottom took the plunge in front of spectators in London, England, and earned himself a place in the record books for his splashing feat!

31

Hide and Seek

A British woman sparked a full-scale police search, complete with helicopter, for her three-year-old daughter in 2004... when the child was behind a couch the whole time. It was estimated that the search cost £30,000 ($60,000).

Blast Off

Wanting a gas stove for her apartment, a San Francisco woman stole one from a neighboring building... without first turning off the gas. She caused a $200,000 explosion.

Double Bass

Arthur K. Ferris of Ironia, New Jersey, built a 14-ft (4.25-m) high bass fiddle.

Break a Leg

Charles Grubbs and Melody Wyman had set their hearts on being married at the top of Mount Rainier, Washington State, but on their way up the mountain for the 2002 ceremony, high winds blew them and their minister into a crevasse. After a visit to hospital, the wedding went ahead as planned… except that the bride had a plaster cast on her leg and needed the aid of a crutch.

Blank Looks

A counterfeiter in Paramount, California, did a sterling job preparing fake notes that he tried to pass on to a store owner. There was just one giveaway: the back of the bills was completely blank.

What a Giveaway

Los Angeles police got lucky with a robbery suspect who just couldn't keep his mouth shut. When detectives asked each man in the line-up to repeat the words, "Give me all your money or I'll shoot," the guilty man shouted: "That's not what I said!"

Breaking the Ice

Sri Lankan farmer Gamini Wasantha Kumara endured having no fewer than 50 blocks of ice dropped on him from a height of 17 ft (5 m). Gamini laid with a block of granite weighing 440 lb (200 kg) on his chest, while the blocks of ice, each weighing a further 110 lb (50 kg), were dropped on top of him, one at a time.

A Real Cliff-hanger

Eskil Ronningsbakken performing his trademark handstand without a safety net 2,000 ft (600 m) above sea level at Pulpit Cliff, Norway.

Hit the Roof

Extreme artist Eskil Ronningsbakken does a handstand on top of the 280-ft (86-m) high Radisson S.A.S. Scandinavia Building in Copenhagen, Denmark.

ERICSSO

Between a Rock and a Hard Place

No stranger to heights or handstands, Eskil Ronningsbakken balances on four stacked chairs at more than 3,000 ft (1,000 m) above sea level in Norway.

When You're in a Hole...

After six months of digging a secret tunnel from Saltillo Prison, Mexico, 75 convicts made their daring bid for freedom, only to find that their tunnel emerged in the nearby courtroom where many of them had been sentenced. The surprised judges quickly sent them back to jail.

Mummy's Boy

A 22-year-old Los Angeles man advertised in a magazine as a lonely Romeo looking for a girl to accompany him on vacation to South America. Alas, the first reply he received turned out to be from his widowed mother!

Badge of Dishonor

A would-be robber of a Texas grocery store disguised his face with a balaclava, but forgot to remove from his breast pocket a laminated badge that bore his name, place of employment, and position within the company—an oversight spotted by witnesses.

Lost in Translation

An elderly American tourist had to be rescued from woodland in Bavaria, Germany, in 2004 after he got lost while using a 90-year-old guidebook.

Get your Facts Straight

A woman from Connecticut was identified in 2003 as the person who had robbed six banks after she called her local newspaper to complain about inaccuracies in their reports of her robberies.

Seed Drill

Taiwanese artist Chen Forng-Shean wrote this 28-character poem by ancient Chinese poet Su Tung-po on a sesame seed! When the seed is placed on the face of George Washington on a $1 note, the scale of the writing can be fully appreciated.

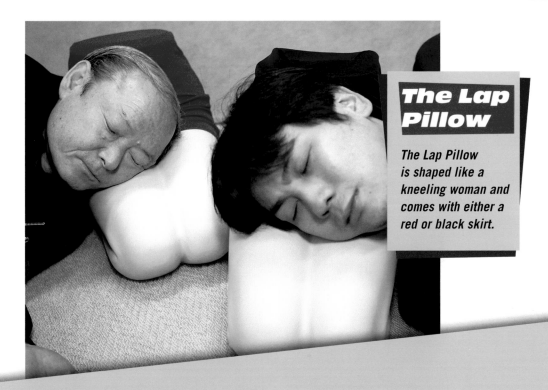

The Lap Pillow

The Lap Pillow is shaped like a kneeling woman and comes with either a red or black skirt.

It's in the Bag

Hoping to look inconspicuous, a bank robber in Portland, Oregon, handed the teller a note ordering her to put all the money in a paper bag. She read the note, wrote on the bottom, "I don't have a paper bag," and handed it back to the raider. His plan foiled, he fled empty-handed.

What's the Hold-up?

A man robbed a bank in Briarwood, West Virginia, in 2004 by taping a "stick-up" note to the teller's window. He was arrested when he later returned to the same window because he had forgotten to pick up the note!

Emergency Service

Policemen who arrested a burglar on the roof of a bank in Kent, England, had to be rescued by fire crews after they became stuck.

In the Hot Seat

Around the time of the invention of the electric chair, an unwitting citizen in New York State offered to test the electric current in the chair: the current worked, the man died, and the man's family received $5,000.

Turn Yourself In

After robbing an Ohio convenience store in 2004, a man hijacked a car and led police on a high-speed chase before taking a wrong turn and driving into a police station parking lot.

A Night to Remember

Residents of the Romanian village of Cristinesti fled their homes in panic in 2004 after mistaking disco lights in a nearby town for an alien invasion!

Finger of Fate

A man in Modesto, California, was arrested for trying to hold up a Bank of America branch without a weapon. He used a thumb and finger to simulate a gun, but forgot to keep his hand in his pocket.

Airline Food

A group of vintage aviation enthusiasts left their plane in a field near Hereford, England, while they went to lunch in a nearby pub. When they returned, they found the 1948 Auster airplane being eaten by cows! The animals caused thousands of pounds worth of damage by chewing a large hole in the fuselage.

No Strings Attached

Contortionist Captain Frodo, a member of the Circus Oz, dislocates certain bones in his body to enable him to pass his body through a tennis racket as part of his performance!

Barbie World

As part of a promotion for Barbie, all the houses in this street in Manchester, England, were temporarily painted bright pink!

A Hiding to Nothing

A Romanian man sentenced for fraud in 1994 hid in his parents' basement for eight years—to avoid a three-and-a-half-year jail sentence.

Unlucky Number

Sentenced to seven years in jail, a man from San Antonio, Texas, begged the judge not to give him seven years because seven was his unlucky number. So the judge gave him eight years.

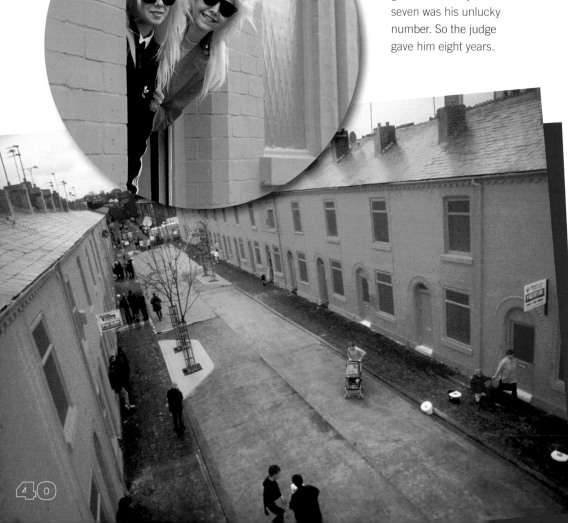

Stone the Crows!

Mistaking it for a Viking settlement, archeologists excavated an ordinary 1940s patio in a back garden in Fife, Scotland.

Other Fish to Fry

Firefighters in Baton Rouge, Louisiana, burned down their own fire station after leaving fish frying on a stove when they were called out to attend a blaze.

Caught Out

Two burglars fled from a building in Florida in 2003 and jumped into what they thought was their getaway car, only to find that it was an unmarked police car!

A Nasty Shock

A man in Kitwe, Zambia, was electrocuted in 2000 when, having run out of space on his clothes line, he unwisely decided to hang the remainder of his wet washing on a live power line that passed his house.

Double Trouble

A year after crashing into Jim Hughes' yacht near Portsmouth, England, and causing £20,000 ($40,000)

damage, Icelandic sailor Eriker Olafsson still felt guilty. So he decided to return to the harbor and make a full apology, only to hit Mr Hughes' yacht again and postpone his plans for a round-the-world voyage for a second time!

Courtroom Drama

A computer error resulted in an eight-year-old boy from New Jersey being summoned for jury service in 2001. It was the second time Kyle Connor had been called up to serve on a jury, the first being when he was five. Kyle said he was perfectly happy to try it, as long as the judge didn't mind!

Triumphant Stag

An American poacher who shot a stag standing above him on an overhanging rock was killed instantly when the dead animal fell on him.

Wind Break

Frank Morosky of Cedar Rapids, Iowa, has made charcoal-lined diapers costing between $20 and $50, to reduce the odor of dogs' flatulence.

Puss in... Slippers

Japanese inventor Kenji Kawakami has conceived a pair of duster slippers to be worn by a cat, so that the animal can polish the floor while it walks!

On the Record

A pair of agitated robbers burst into a record store in Michigan, nervously waving guns. One shouted: "Nobody move!" When his accomplice moved, the first bandit shot him.

Bare-faced Cheek

A Canadian man who was refused a ticket from Los Angeles to Australia in 2004, took off all his clothes, ran naked across the runway, and climbed into a plane's wheel well. Firefighters finally talked him out.

Heavy Duty

Weighing 147 lb (67 kg), Stephen Stoyan made two successive push-ups with 285 lb (129 kg) on his back.

The Party's Over

After a party in 2001, a woman fell asleep on a mattress in an Alabama garbage bin… and woke hours later in a Georgia landfill 20 mi (30 km) away. She narrowly escaped being crushed by a garbage compactor.

Tooth and Nail

A dentist soon got to the root of Patrick Lawler's toothache—a 4-in (10-cm) nail that the construction worker had embedded in his skull six days earlier! A nail gun had backfired while he was working at a Colorado ski resort, sending one nail into a piece of wood, and another through his mouth and 1½ in (4 cm) into his brain.

A Cut Above

Joe Horowitz from Los Angeles was able to balance an 18-lb (8-kg) saber on the end of his nose!

Pressing the Limits

Rev. Jon Bruney from Fremont, Indiana, performs exhibitions of strength as part of his "Pressing the Limits" event.

His strongman activities include breaking flaming bricks, crushing a full can of soda, and inflating a hot-water bottle until it explodes. In July 2004, Jon was one of three strongmen to pull a 15-ton semi-tractor trailer for a distance of 1 mi (1.5 km)! The trailer was loaded with the band Bledsoe, who performed on the flatbed of the truck.

"Little Giant" Eddie Polo

Tearing his Hair Out

"Little Giant" Eddie Polo pulls a car 100 yd (90 m) in 1 minute 40 seconds in Dover, New Hampshire, in August 1937—using only the strength of his hair.

Growing Room
A German firm has developed a shoe that grows to keep pace with children's feet. At the press of a button, the shoe increases by one size by expanding like an accordion.

A Lost Cause
A tourist from Toledo, Washington, on holiday in Germany in 2003, relied solely on his car's automatic navigation system to steer him around the unfamiliar roads of Bavaria… until it led him straight through the doors of a supermarket. The tourist, who said he didn't even see the supermarket doors, came to a halt when he crashed into a row of shelves.

On the Fiddle
Ontario police charged a motorist with careless driving after catching him playing the violin while at the wheel. The 54-year-old man said he was warming up for a concert.

Economy Drive
Resenting the prospect of paying a $55 delivery fee on his new lawnmower, a man from Plainville, Connecticut, decided instead to drive it home along the road at a top speed of 12 mph (20 km/h). Far from saving money, he was fined $78 for driving an unregistered vehicle!

46

Having a Ball

The Stade de France stadium in Paris was transformed into a beach in July 2002 with 100,000 sq ft (9,000 sq m) of sand. Visitors could play ball games or simply relax in deckchairs.

Life's a Beach

One bank of the River Seine is turned into a beach each summer so that Parisians can enjoy the sunshine without having to trek to the coast. The mayor had the "Paris Plage" developed to include palm trees, sand, and a swimming pool.

47

Heaven Scent

These rose-scented stamps were used on letters in Thailand in 2002. Printed in England, they were released in Bangkok in February to commemorate St. Valentine's Day.

A Change of Key

Frankie Masters had a 12-strong band, with a difference—each member played music on a manual typewriter. The overall effect sounded like a xylophone.

Banana Split

A Cincinnati-based firm is planning to market strawberry-flavored bananas! Chiquita International claims bananas taste boring.

The Name of the Game

When Californian artist Maria Alquilar painted a $40,000 mural outside a public library, little did she realize that it contained 11 misspelled names of historical giants including Shakespeare, Einstein, Van Gogh, and Michelangelo. It is thought to have cost around $6,000 to correct the mistakes.

O Brother!

Acting as his own lawyer in a Texas federal court, Adam Martin called his brother to the witness stand to testify to his good character. When Adam asked his brother if he had ever committed any crimes, his brother responded without hesitation: "Yeah. You were with me on four different bank robberies, Adam. You know that."

I Want to Ride My Tricycle

Bobby Jordan and six of his friends, who call themselves the "Descanso Big Wheel Boys," consider themselves Big Wheel daredevils—despite being adults. For the last year, the full-grown men have been getting their thrills by racing their toy tricycles down steep California mountainsides. They typically reach 35 mph (55 km/h), which causes the plastic wheels to disintegrate long before they reach the bottom.

Brace Yourself

Truck driver Herbert Scott from Burnley, England, in 1986 sought medical attention following a fall at work. As a result of a misunderstanding, he kept a neck brace on for the next 14 years instead of the four weeks that the doctors had advised.

Fire Drill

When fire broke out at a restaurant in the Austrian city of Vienna in November 2003, the owner and staff quickly fled the building. In their haste, they forgot to evacuate the guests. Even though the dining room had filled with smoke, 20 people were still sitting at their tables when fire crews arrived.

Bird-brained

Thieves who stole 15 homing pigeons from bird-fancier Peter Ball of Berkshire, England, tried them out… and watched in despair as they flew straight back to Ball's loft!

These lucky pups are now looked after by gardener Henry Escott, who ensures that they have everything they need.

The Color of Money

An unemployed American printer who turned to counterfeiting was caught because he used black ink instead of bright green on his phoney bills. It turned out that he was color-blind.

Dozy Burglar

It was bad enough that a burglar chose to break into the offices of the police department in Oxnard, California, but to make matters worse, he then fell asleep! Bemused police discovered him when they arrived for work in the morning, and promptly made him the first arrest of the day.

Going to the Dogs

Tina and Kate, two dogs living in Somerset, England, inherited £450,000 ($900,000) when their owner passed away. The inheritance was enough for them to be able to enjoy a home and 4 acre (1.6 ha) of land in the village of Peasedown St. John.

Does It Bite?

Phones, like this one by Mauro Caputo, were exhibited and later auctioned at "Show and Tel: the Art of Connection," held at the Zimmer Children's Museum in Los Angeles, California.

Zimmer Frame

"Commander Ian Zimmer," designed by Alan and Deborah Ladwig, is just one of the bizarre telephonic inventions that were on display.

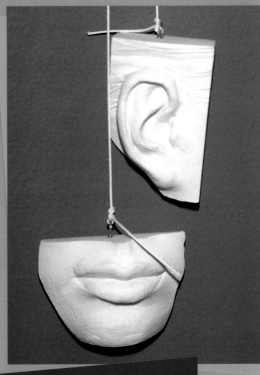

I'm All Ears

The exhibition included quirky designs such as this two-part ear-and-mouthpiece telephone by Robert Graham.

Ring My Bell

Wedding bells won't be the only bells ringing on this telephone, created by Jessica Trovato. The designers of the unusual creations at the exhibition included athletes, politicians, and celebrities, such as Elizabeth Taylor, Alicia Keys, and Paula Abdul.

Strong Man

Jon Bruney bends a steel bar against the top of his head, during one of his motivational performances.

To illustrate his sheer strength, Jon is able to tear entire phone books in half!

Fall Guy

Brazilian Marcello Bonga made the first ever crossing by rope of the Iguazu waterfalls from the Brazilian side to the Argentinian side. He crossed the Devil's Throat section, using only a rope and a harness, as thousands of tons of water crashed beneath him.

Life in The Fast Lane

Wheel of Fire

Known as "Pyro Boy," website designer
Wally Glenn's life is a hotbed of flames!

Pyro Boy designed his own helmet and outfit, which were made from fire-retardant material.

Pyro Boy bravely walks through rings of fire. He did it once and was unharmed, but another time he caught fire!

Wally Glenn walks through rings of flames, wearing a fire-retardant suit, and with explosives strapped to his body. At a death-defying event at Ripley's Aquarium in Myrtle Beach, South Carolina, in November 1999, Pyro Boy braved temperatures as high as 2,000°F (1,100°C).

Once inside the suit, Pyro Boy had 20 lb (9 kg) of explosives strapped to his body.

The event was more than just a flash in the pan: it was recorded for the Ripley television show in November 1999.

With temperatures reaching as high as 2,000°F (1,100°C) outside the suit, it's no surprise that Pyro Boy's neck was singed beneath his suit.

59

Pole Position

Jenefer Davies Mansfield, a choreographer, staged her NASCAR Ballet at a Virginia theater in 2003. The production featured 20 dancers clad in corporate patches of the theater's sponsors. As they leaped around a banked-racetrack stage, occasionally crashing into each other, the dancers were accompanied by the sounds of revving engines. Mansfield hoped to entice NASCAR fans who were in the area for race day.

Tall Order

In 1989, Randall Jones of Georgia built what is believed to be the world's tallest bicycle. It stands at 17 ft 2 in (5 m) tall. The diameter of the front wheel is 26 ft (8 m).

The Car's the Star

Some of the strangest looking vehicles in America can be found at the Art Car Museum in Houston, Texas. Eccentric owners have decorated their cars to reflect their personalities, covering them in everything from buttons and pennies, to grass and flowers. Among the most colorful exhibits are the Roachster, a vehicle decorated like a cockroach; the Swamp Mutha, adorned with birds and curious creatures; Faith, which has a buffalo head at the front of the car; and Rex Rabbit, a car designed in the shape of a huge rabbit.

On the Rocks

The Princess May, which ran aground in 1910 on Sentinel Island, Alaska, during a low tide, rose 30 ft (9 m) in the air! Tugs eventually pulled the vessel from the rocks.

PRINCESS MAY

You Shall Go to the Ball!

Originally a boat that was used to sail the canals of Venice, this wooden Cinderella's carriage has been converted into a roadworthy vehicle—it's even been used as a wedding carriage.

Crash Test Dummy

A Toronto teenager crashed into six cars as she completed the parking maneuver of her 2001 driving test. She was all set to pass until she turned into the parking lot of the test center, and accidentally pressed the accelerator instead of the brake, hitting the cars.

Emergency Exit

When 41-year-old Fidel Cueva decided to exit a Greyhound bus window, it didn't seem to matter to him that the bus was traveling at 55 mph (90 km/h) through rush-hour traffic. Perhaps it was because he was so upset that the express bus had just bypassed his stop.

Supply and Demand

Hyperactive Technologies, a company based in Pittsburgh, currently offers software to fast-food restaurants that predicts customer rushes. The "Hyperactive Bob" system predicts demand using rooftop cameras that monitor traffic entering the eateries' parking lots and drive-thru lanes. By the end of 2005, however, restaurant managers should be able to access software that predicts what customers will actually order—based on the vehicle that they drive.

You Win Some...

Dennis L. Wheat, from Malvern, Arkansas, won his car in a raffle. Unluckily for him, however, he later discovered that it was the same car he had traded-in six years earlier!

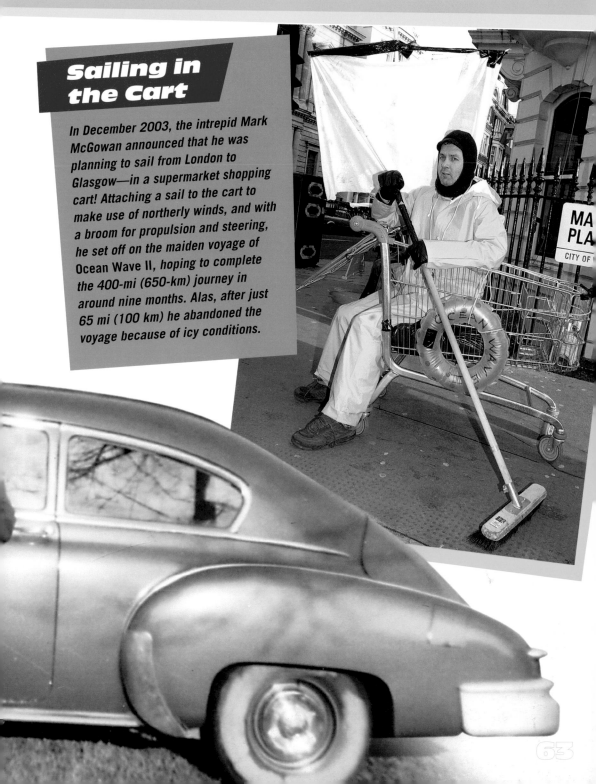

Sailing in the Cart

In December 2003, the intrepid Mark McGowan announced that he was planning to sail from London to Glasgow—in a supermarket shopping cart! Attaching a sail to the cart to make use of northerly winds, and with a broom for propulsion and steering, he set off on the maiden voyage of *Ocean Wave II*, hoping to complete the 400-mi (650-km) journey in around nine months. Alas, after just 65 mi (100 km) he abandoned the voyage because of icy conditions.

MA
PLA
CITY OF

How Low Can You Go?

Andy Saunders has customized his 1985 Mini in a unique way—by making it the lowest in the world. The mini Mini is just 34 in (86 cm) high.

End of the Line

In 2001, more than 400 New York subway cars were pushed into the sea by a bulldozer off Cape Hanlopen, Delaware. They landed 80 ft (25 m) under the surface of the Atlantic. The aim was to create an artificial reef, attracting more fish.

The Bicycle Thief

Ken James of Melbourne, Australia, died when he fell off a bicycle he had stolen. Police found more than 400 stolen bikes at his home.

Way to Mow!

Gary Hatter of Champaign, Illinois, made a 14,500-mi (23,000-km) journey around America—on a lawnmower! Leaving Portland, Maine, in May 2000, he passed through all 48 continuous U.S. states and dipped into Canada and Mexico, before arriving at Daytona Beach, Florida, in February 2001. One of his proudest moments came halfway through the 260 days of riding when, in Iowa, he overtook another vehicle!

Boy Racer

Robb Lapeen from Flint, Michigan, jumped over nine cars on his motorbike—when he was just eight years old. He has been riding motorbikes since he was two and first raced on ice and dirt at the age of four.

WINDY CITY

Full of Hot Air

This monster truck was created by Scottish balloon artist Colin Myles in 2003. Colin has made all sorts of sculptures from balloons, such as a liquorice man, a giant sunflower, and animals including bears and kangaroos.

Wheely Slow

A 73-year-old Milwaukee man irked motorists by traveling on the highway at 5 mph (8 km/h)—in his wheelchair. Despite the fact that wheelchairs aren't allowed on the highway, the man took his chances after a transportation service failed to pick him up for his doctor's appointment.

Starting Young

In 2003, after the keys had been left in the ignition of Taccara King's pickup, her two-year-old son started it and crashed it into a transport office at Vero Beach, Florida.

Pedal Power

Grand Prix rules apply in an annual pedal-powered car race. Competitors race around streets in Valentigney, France, with drivers and cars in costume: recent races have seen banana cars with monkey drivers and pumpkin cars with witches at the wheel. The winner is judged on the basis of both speed and costume.

Put Your Foot on the Gas

Roman Kunikov, a Russian professor, has designed gasoline-powered boots. Tests in a public square at Ufa, near Moscow, showed that wearers could achieve speeds of up to 25 mph (40 km/h).

Baling Out

In 2003, in Makoti, North Dakota, John Smith, also known as the "Flying Farmer," jumped his car over 25 bales of hay—covering a total distance of 160 ft (50 m). John had told his wife earlier that year that if he hadn't sold the hay bales by the start of February, he would jump over them in his car.

Rock Lobster

The Art Car Weekend, held annually in Houston, Texas, attracts a host of unusual vehicles, including this cute crustacean.

A Barrel of Laughs

Speeds of up to 15 mph (25 km/h) can be reached by these wacky racers of beer kegs, in Windsor, England.

Coining It!

You could say that Ken Burkitt of Niagara Falls, Ontario, Canada, is money mad!

Ken's obsession with coins is not confined to his wallet—he has decorated several cars with coins and he spends his time making sure he covers every inch of each vehicle. Ken covered this Mini and a limousine with thousands of coins. All of the cars Ken has decorated are in full working order—in fact, they are in mint condition! Each coin that Ken uses is covered with at least eight coats of polyurethane, in order to stop it from discoloring or rusting.

Ripley's —
COIN-COVERED MINI
EXHIBIT NO: 11647
1969 AUSTIN MINI
COVERED IN GOLD-PLATED
ENGLISH PENNIES

The coins are bent into shape using a vice to make them cover every inch of the car.

Gold-plated English pennies cover this 1988 Lincoln Continental stretch limousine, part of the Ripley collection.

The mid-1980s MGB Roadster, which is covered in gold-plated English pennies, is currently on display at the Ripley's Museum in Mexico.

Talking Turkey

Josh Harper overslept on Christmas Day 2002 and had to drive to his girlfriend's house for dinner, so he decided to cook the turkey on his car engine while he traveled the 90 mi (145 km) to her home in Bristol, England. "The potatoes were a little firm," he said, "but the turkey was done to a treat."

Higher Car

Gary Duval of Colton, California, has built a car that measures 10 ft 11 in (3 m) high from the ground to the roof. It sits on eight monster truck tires, has two separate engines, and took more than 4,000 hours to build.

Tug of Love

In 2000, 20 men pulled an 18-ton dump truck around a parking lot in Kenosha, Wisconsin, for an hour without stopping. By the end, they had pulled the truck a total distance of 3⅛ mi (5 km).

Sticky Situation

A West Virginia woman was literally glued to the floor, when she didn't realize that the 3M liquid bandage she had applied to her heel had dripped down to her toes. Family members had to call 911, and three paramedics took more than an hour and a bottle of baby oil to free her. The woman said the humiliation of still being in her robe was by far the worst part of the experience.

Toilet Roll

In 1999, Hank Harp drove a motorized toilet the length of Britain—a total of 874 mi (1,300 km). He sat on the seat of the chemical toilet, which was powered by an electric motor and had a top speed of 4 mph (6 km/h), and stored the supplies that he needed for his journey in the bowl.

Hamburger Harley

Harry Sperl rides around Daytona Beach, Florida, with relish—on an 1100 cc Harley-Davidson trike that has been covered with a huge Fiberglass-and-Styrofoam hamburger. The Hamburger Harley comes with a melting-cheese fender and ketchup-bottle shock covers. Harry's love for bikes is matched only by his passion for burgers. He also owns the world's only Hamburger Museum.

Starring Rolls

Graham Crossley of Sheffield, England, is crazy about Rolls-Royces—even though he can't drive. The 41-year-old has been in love with Rollers since the age of 11. He has a collection of more than 2,500 photographs, tours garages, and often spends his weekends washing other people's Rolls-Royces for nothing—just so that he can get close to his favorite cars.

Sign of the Times

Confused by a Los Angeles freeway sign, artist Richard Ankrom took matters into his own hands in 2001. He scaled the sign and added a vital direction so well that state officials were unable to detect the alteration. After tracking down the authentic reflective buttons that make up each letter from a company in Tacoma, Washington, he added the helpful word "north" to the sign. While making the change, he wore a hard hat and orange fluorescent vest to avert suspicion.

High-flyer

Setting the world record for the highest human flight with a rocket belt, American stunt expert Eric Scott reached a height of 152 ft (46 m). He strapped the rocket belt around his waist and, with the aid of the jetpack on his back, took off in the skies over London in 2004.

On his Knees

Australian charity worker Suresh Joachim attempted to break the world record for a continuous crawl in 2001. The current record, which was set in 1992, stands at 31⅓ mi (50.5 km). To break this, Joachim needed to complete 2,500 laps of his enclosure on the streets of Sydney, Australia.

Milking it

Sam Draper and Julie Magenis of Houston, Texas, have turned a 1979 Cadillac into the Cow-de-lac. Painted black and white like a Friesian cow, the car has an Astroturf interior and upholstery made from feed and potato sacks. The hood is adorned with model cows while the roof displays a farmyard scene.

Revving up

English vicar Rev. Paul Sinclair, also known as the "Faster Pastor," has a sidecar hearse on his motorcycle so that he can give deceased bikers a suitable send-off. It cost £30,000 ($60,000) to convert his 955 cc machine, which can hold a coffin at speeds of up to 70 mph (115 km/h).

RIPLEY's
STICK ROLLS ROYCE
EXHIBIT NO: 13081
TOOK 4,609 HOURS TO COMPLETE, AND MEASURES 12 FT 8 IN (4 M) IN LENGTH

Jump to it

Texan parachutist Mike Zang managed to jump out of a plane 500 times in less than 24 hours over Fort Worth, Texas, in May 2001. This means he achieved an average of one parachute jump every three minutes, despite mechanical problems, lightning, and heavy rain.

My Hands Are Tied

In 2004, Italian Alberto Cristini swam the 2 mi (3 km) from the island of Alcatraz to San Francisco in 1 hour, 50 minutes—with his hands and feet tied together! Fighting strong currents, Alberto made it through the freezing cold stretch of water. The race was pioneered in 1955 by fitness guru Jack La Lanne, who did it while wearing handcuffs.

Plane Stupid

Louis Kadlecek had never flown a plane, but stole a two-seater Cessna from an airport in Houston, Texas, and flew for about a mile before crashing into electricity lines. Mr. Kadlecek was unhurt and walked home after the accident, before being arrested by police.

Just Deserts

The Baja 1,000 Desert Race takes place every November. It's a test of endurance, during which car drivers have been known to cover the very bumpy 1,000-mi (1,500-km) course with broken bones. Ivan "Ironman" Stewart completed the course in just 20 hours in 1998.

The Flip Side

At the Gravity Games in Rhode Island, in 2002, Carey Hart performed a back flip on a motorbike, traveling 20 ft (6 m) before landing. It was the first recorded back flip on a full-size bike.

Pulling Power

In 1990, bodybuilder Georges Christen decided to test his pulling power by holding on to ropes attached to three light aircraft as they attempted to take off.

Not in my Backyard

Back in 1969, when he was still studying at high school, Kim Pedersen made the initial sketches of a monorail he wanted to build in his backyard. Unsurprisingly, his parents dismissed the whole idea, but now that Kim has a place of his own, he has finally been able to realize his dream. Consequently, his home in Fremont, California, is probably the only one in the world with a working monorail in the backyard. The track runs 300 ft (90 m) around the perimeter of his backyard and is 8 ft (2.4 m) tall at its highest point. The monorail took five years to construct, at a cost of $4,000, but monorail-mad Kim reckons it's worth every cent!

The Fastest Milkman in the West

Welsh racing-driver Richard Rozhon established the inaugural world speed record for the electric milk float. He managed to get the humble machine to accumulate 73 mph (117 km/h) at a milk-float speed trial in Leicestershire, England, in 2003.

Way to Go

The Appian Way, which originally connected Rome, Italy, with Capua, was so well built that it is still in use after more than 2,000 years. The 4-ft (1-m) thick highway, which is more than 350 mi (550 km) long, would cost more than $500,000 a mile to build today.

The Jet Set

The latest pastime for thrill-seeking adrenalin junkies on the Caribbean island of St. Marten is to stand on the beach at the end of the runway at Princess Juliana International Airport and try to remain upright as the huge airplanes take off. People have been tossed in the air by the sheer force of the planes flying so low overhead.

First-class Lounge

As a nine-year-old boy, Gregory Langley always flew first-class—because he had a seat from his favorite plane, Concorde, installed in his home.

Destined for Great Heights

At ten years old Paul Hill could have been the world's youngest pilot, and he was certainly the youngest boy in England ever to fly a plane.

After watching his father, Terry, take flying lessons, Paul soon picked up the necessary skills, although he couldn't fly solo until he turned 17.

Paul successfully flew a Cessna 150—with a qualified co-pilot.

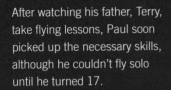

Paul's dream to fly Concorde may not have come true, but he was delighted with his successful take-offs and landings.

Head Over Heels

This giant stiletto was built in the Philippines around a 1,000 cc Japanese motorbike.

City of Marikina

Motorized Cycle Footwear

WORK HARD
WORK WELL
WORK TOGETHER

ANOTHER PROJECT OF
ENGINEERING DEPARTMENT
MOTORPOOL SECTION

Tanks Very Much

An Austrian soldier was fined for speeding… in a 25-ton tank. Even though he was on a military exercise, the soldier had to pay the fine for driving at 40 mph (60 km/h) within a 30 mph (50 km/h) zone.

Beer Necessities

After a heavy snowstorm in 2001, police in Grand Island, Nebraska, reported that a man stole a snowplow from a Hastings storage shed and drove it 20 mi (30 km)—just to buy a case of beer.

Going Flat Out

In 1995, Dutch cyclist Fred Rompelberg achieved the highest ever recorded speed on a bicycle—more than 167 mph (269 km/h)—at Bonneville Salt Flats, Utah.

78

Breaking Step

The San Francisco Bay to Breakers foot race attracts up to 75,000 runners, many of them in a variety of costumes such as giant chickens, Batman, and sets of dominoes.

In the Name of the Lawn

The National Lawnmower Racing Championships take place in Mendota, Illinois. The race started out as an April Fools' joke in 1992, but has proved so popular that it has become an annual event.

Keeping his Cool

In February 2000, actor Paul Newman became the world's oldest racing driver when he competed at the Daytona International Speedway in Florida. He was 75 years and 11 days old on the day—and his co-driver was just 17.

Space Race

The crew of the command module Apollo 10 became the fastest human beings ever when the module reached 24,791 mph (39,900 km/h).

Self-build

Measuring 19 ft 4 in (6 m) in length and weighing 2,800 lb (1,270 kg), this Longhorn V-12 took Texan Oliver Albert 12 years to build—by hand! Oliver built it using the best parts of more than 14 different types of vehicle—including a Cadillac, Chevrolet, Chrysler, Dodge, Ford, Jeep, Lincoln, Mercedes, Mercury, Nash, Plymouth, Pontiac, Renault, and Terraplane.

WORLD'S SNAZZIEST SPORT ROADSTER
LONGHORN — V-12 — CUSTOM BUILT — OLIVER ALBERT - GONZALES, TEXAS

You Wanna Jet?

Andy Green reached an amazing 763 mph (1,228 km/h) in Thrust, his twin-jet-engine supersonic car, in October 1997. He established a world land-speed record at the event in the Black Rock Desert, Nevada.

Another Fine Mess

A massive speeding fine of more than $200,000 was issued to millionaire Jussi Salonoja in Finland in 2004. The amount was calculated to reflect Mr. Salonoja's large income.

Reach for the Skies

The annual run up the Empire State Building has imitators all over the world, including a run up the monumental Petronas Towers in Malaysia.

Table Mountain

The Annual Furniture Race in Whitefish, Montana, involves competitors attaching skis to various items of furniture and racing down the nearby Big Mountain.

From the Bottom to ZZ Top

Depicting many world-famous musicians—including ZZ Top, Madonna, Jimi Hendrix, and Sir Elton John—the creators intended to purvey the message "music lives forever." The car is decorated with sculpted styrofoam, and covered with beads, glass, jewelry, and albums.

RIPLEY'S

"GRATEFUL UNDEAD"
EXHIBIT NO: 21480
CREATED BY HOUSTON ART
TEACHER REBECCA BASS AND
19 ART STUDENTS

Recycled Cycles

In the 1930s, Joseph Steinlauf, a mechanic from Chicago, Illinois, created bicycles made from all sorts of material, including guns, a sewing machine, and even an old headboard and a hot-water bottle! The gun bicycle weighed about 350 lb (160 kg).

It's a Knockout

In November 2004, Romanian Alin Popescu stole a car and then crashed into a tree and knocked himself out after traveling half a mile. He was lucky not to have been killed, especially as he is blind.

One Careful Owner

Retired science teacher Irvin Gordon of East Patchogue, New York, drives a 1966 Volvo P1800S that has well over 2 million mi (3 million km) on the clock—the highest mileage recorded by any car in the world. Irvin has been the car's only owner—he bought it new in June 1966. He used to commute 125 mi (200 km) to work every day, and loves his car so much that since he retired he often drives to other states for lunch.

Engine Room

Two production cars that were built in the early 20th century hold the record for the largest engine capacity. The Peerless 6-60, which was built between 1912 and 1914, and the Fageol, which was built in 1918, both had 13.5-liter engines.

Dead Heat

Manitou Springs, Colorado, is famous for its annual coffin races, in which competitors zoom down the town's main street in wheeled coffins.

Going on a Bender

Uri Geller became famous as a spoon-bending psychic. His art car, called "The Geller Effect," is a Cadillac completely covered with thousands of pieces of bent cutlery.

Hitting the Roof

A Massachusetts man was getting ready for his Fourth of July cookout when the fireworks started early: a Ford Taurus drove off an elevated parking lot and crashed through the roof of his house. No one was hurt in the freak accident, but guests were surprised to see the car sticking out of the roof when they arrived to begin the celebrations.

A Dream Wedding

A bride's dream of a memorable wedding came true when she arrived at the ceremony in a four-poster bed on wheels. Lisa Turner followed groom Simon Croft, who traveled in a mobile office, complete with boardroom table and water cooler, in a bizarre 5-mi (8-km) procession in Hampshire, England, in 2004.

A Fishy Business

If you ask Singapore businessman Lawrence Ng what's in the tank of his Jaguar, the answer is simple: fish. By ripping out the seats and engine, and sealing the windows and doors, he has converted his car into a big fish tank. The trunk and hood are home to filter systems and air pumps, and the fish are fed through the sunroof.

Judge Dread

Officials in Mount Holly, New Jersey, decided to introduce humorous road signs because the conventional kind were not

Good Day at the Office, Dear?

Swapping desks was taken to new extremes when Edd China invented the world's first "office car." The roadworthy workspace made its debut in London, England, in 2003, at the start of a 900-mi (1,500-km) charity road trip to the South of France.

He Sure Can Carry a Note

J. Clark Cullom, of Cincinnati, Ohio, carried a piano with him wherever he went! He traveled more than 15,000 mi (24,000 km) with it strapped to his car.

proving to be effective enough. The colorful signs bear messages such as "Meet Our Judge—Exceed 25 mph (40 km/h)" and "Free Speeding Tickets Ahead."

Rocket Man

By fitting 24 rockets to his luge, a light toboggan, Billy Copeland of Ashland City, Tennessee, can reach speeds of nearly 100 mph (160 km/h) in just six seconds on steep hills.

All Aboard!

All 34 members of India's Army Services Corps Tornadoes go for a spin on an Indian-built Enfield Bullet 500 cc motorcycle in Bangalore in June 2004.

Bouncing Babies

In a freak accident, two young toddlers fell three stories from a Los Angeles apartment window—and lived. The resilient toddlers were taken to the hospital to be checked out, but soon recovered.

Dead Man Walking

Despite the fact that his family thought he'd been hit by a train, Dane Squires of Toronto was very much alive—and in the dark about arrangements for his funeral service. He called his daughter's cell phone just as his casket was

being loaded into a hearse, causing her to freak out, believing his ghost was trying to contact her. The man's sister had previously identified the dead body to be his.

Wheels on Fire

Roller-blading was no easy task back in 1906. Inventor Alphonse Constantini invented motor-driven skates—they could travel at up to 40 mph (64 km/h).

Wind Tunnel

Slow riders in the Netherlands needn't worry—there is an 8-mi (13-km) long tunnel that contains massive electric fans—they push along riders at up to 28 mph (45 km/h).

Blind Ambition

Being blind hasn't stopped Mike Newman setting speed records. He set the first world record for unsighted driving on a motorbike at 89 mph (143 km/h) in 2001. Then, in 2003, he broke the record for unsighted driving when he reached 144 mph (232 km/h) in a Jaguar XJR.

Bag of Tricks

Indian magician O.P. Sharma drives a motorbike as part of a stunt, with a black bag over his head in August 2004—and it wasn't on an empty road, but a busy street in the city of Patna.

New York Minute

It has been calculated that people in New York travel, on average, a farther distance vertically than they do horizontally. This is owing to the height of the many tall buildings, which makes it necessary to climb more than walk on the level.

A Real Hummer-dinger

It's 39 ft (12 m) long, 8½ ft (2.5 m) wide, and it costs £1,000 ($2,000) a night to hire—it's Britain's longest stretch limousine, a Hummer, owned by Scott Demaret of Bristol.

Wheely Fast

The fastest speed ever achieved on a motorcycle is 322 mph (518 km/h). Dave Campos set the record at Bonneville Salt Flats, Utah, in 1990.

Crash Course

A truck driver deliberately crashed his truck into a parked car outside a bank in Olhsdorf, Austria, thinking it was a getaway vehicle. It wasn't, and the truck driver was liable for repairs and a hefty fine.

The Sky's the Limit

The new Airbus A380 will be the world's largest aircraft when it comes into service in 2007. Its wingspan is nearly 262 ft (80 m), and it stands 80 ft (25 m) tall. The plane will be fitted with casinos, bars, and even gyms for its 555 passengers.

Around the World in 39 Days

Mohammed Salahuddin Choudhury and his wife Neena of Calcutta, India, circumnavigated the Earth by car in just 39 days. They completed their record-breaking journey in Delhi in 1991.

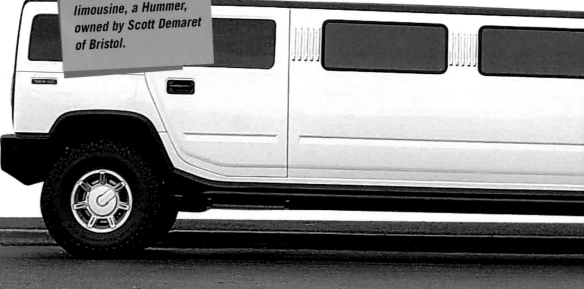

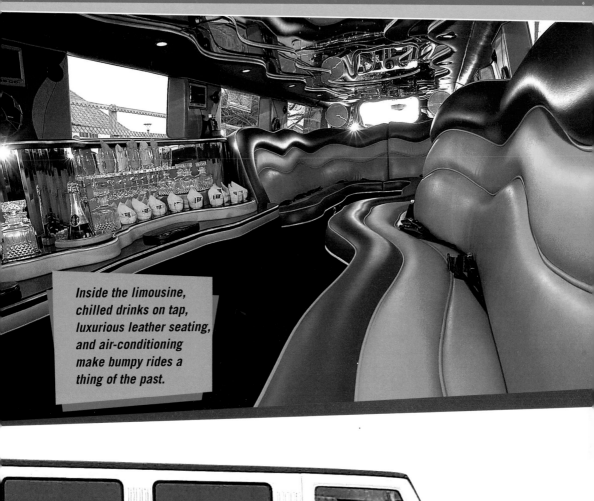

Inside the limousine, chilled drinks on tap, luxurious leather seating, and air-conditioning make bumpy rides a thing of the past.

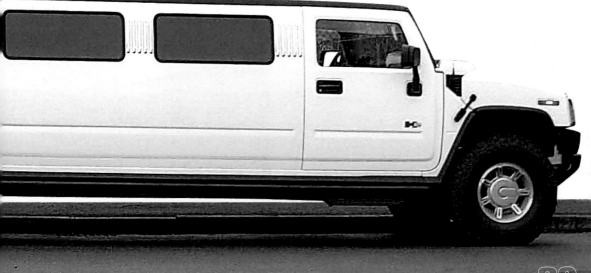

On Home Ground

A river steamer that ran aground off Sauries Island, near Portland, Oregon, was turned into a houseboat.

Race Relations

The island of Tobago hosts annual goat and crab races. Goat jockeys run around the race track alongside the goats, while the crabs are harnessed with string and encouraged along their course by prods from their jockeys.

Pajama Party

Every January, American bed-racing enthusiasts flock to Arizona for the annual Oatman Bed Race. Following a nightwear parade, the teams push their beds down the main street, make their beds, and then race back to the finish line... all to the sweet sounds of the Chamber Pot Band. Even burly bikers have been known to swap their leathers for fluffy pajamas.

Elementary, My Dear Watson

Lloyd Scott, a former British soccer player, used a big-wheeled penny farthing bicycle to cross the continent of Australia in the fall 2004. Scott's 2,700-mi (4,500-km) ride from Perth to Sydney—dressed as Sherlock Holmes—was estimated to have raised almost $2.7 million for charity.

Swims Like a Fish

Brazilian Jose Martins Ribeiro Nunes, who is also known as "Ze Peixe" or "the fish," is 74 years old and leads an exceptionally active life—he guides ships in and out of Brazil's port by swimming along in front of them. He often swims about 8 mi (13 km), in extremely

Golden Wedding

When the Sultan of Brunei's son got married in September 2004, the wedding car was a $20 million, gold-encrusted stretch Rolls-Royce. The luxury car was open-topped to accommodate a double throne for Crown Prince Al-Muhtadee Billah Bolkiah and his bride Sarah Salleh. As even money couldn't buy perfect weather, a golden umbrella was fitted to the car to protect the couple from the rain.

choppy waters, to guide the vessels safely into and out of the harbor! Jose's lifestyle has made him famous on land and at sea, all over the world.

Pump up the Volume

A never-to-be-forgotten family reunion of 55 members—aged from three to 37—was organized by Roger Dumas. Dumas labored for more than 20 years to build a bicycle that could hold them all! During the construction process, he used parts from 150 other bicycles,

but Dumas claimed that the vehicle was built entirely without plans.

Galloping Gourmets

The 26-mi (40-km) course of Le Marathon du Cahors et de la Gastronomie in France is dotted with feeding stations serving foie gras pâté, truffles, and copious quantities of wine. Most competitors are in fancy dress, and the race is followed by a wine festival.

Tanks a Million

On his 265-acre (107-ha) estate, Texas millionaire David Estes used to use 25 military tanks to teach corporate employees leadership through his company, Tactical Tanks. One important lesson participants learned was about communication, because Estes intentionally created chaos, disinformation, and ambiguity in the activities to test them.

Pay Day

It took decades, but an Arizona man has finally paid a $1 parking ticket 38 years after he received it. He found the ticket in an old box that he'd carted around through moves in more than six states and decided it was high time to pay up.

All the Fun of the Fair

Max Tate of Newcastle, England, has converted a fairground bumper car into a street-legal vehicle capable of speeds of 90 mph (145 km/h).

Carted Around

Andy Tyler of Suffolk, England, has created the world's fastest shopping cart—by fitting it with a jet engine! Powered by gas and liquid fuel, it can reach speeds of over 50 mph (80 km/h). There are drawbacks. In order to propel the cart, the engine explodes 40 times a second and is so noisy that it hurts Andy's ears—and he's unlikely ever to be allowed to take it round his local supermarket!

Shoe Tree

On Highway 50 near Middle Gate, Nevada, a lone cottonwood tree is draped with hundreds of pairs of shoes thrown over the branches by passers-by. The first pair are said to have been tossed there during a wedding-night row between young newlyweds.

Going Like a Rocket

Billy Copeland rode his rocket-powered skateboard at 70 mph (113 km/h) in 1998, setting a world record.

Slow Coaches

A group of high school seniors from Indiana drove so slowly in traffic—at approximately 15 mph (25 km/h)—as a prank, that police cited them for reckless driving. The officers were miffed because the students' low speeds caused a 60-car back-up on an Indiana freeway that took them 20 minutes to clear up.

Hair-raising

Entrepreneur Pat Nevin has just the thing for kids to give their parents a shock—his "Hairy Helmets" are colored mohawks that he velcros on to bicycle helmets. He hopes Harley riders might like to try his styles too.

Baby You Can Drive My Car

According to a car survey by Yahoo!Autos, U.S. freeways may be a better place to meet people than weddings or bars, as 62 percent admitted that they love to flirt behind the wheel—and that they are more attracted to those who drive nicer cars.

Disco to Go

Anyone hailing a taxi in Aspen, Colorado, could be in for an unusual journey. Jon Barnes' Ultimate Taxi offers a ride complete with disco ball, smoke machine, strobe lights, lasers, and a dry-ice machine. As if that weren't enough, there's even a drum kit, keyboard, digital camera, and a gift shop in the trunk.

Moving Home

This brick house in Palm Beach, Florida, was donated to a children's charity and moved in one piece to its new location by truck and by barge.

Holy Roller

In the 1970s, it was not unusual to see this mobile church on Britain's roads. The brainchild of one Rev. Dunlop, it was an ordinary bus that was painted to look like a church, complete with a spire sticking out of the roof.

CHURCHMOBILE

Couch Potatoes

It may look like any old sofa, but this one can reach speeds of up to 87 mph (140 km/h)! Licensed for use on U.K. roads, it was created by inventors Edd China and David Davenport, and is powered by a 1300 cc engine. The steering-wheel is made out of a medium-sized pizza pan and the brake pedal is a cola can.

Chainsaws Massacred

This unusual stretch motorbike is powered by 24 chainsaws.

Power Napping

Englishman Edd China specializes in weird vehicles. For £100 ($200), he takes tourists around London on a motorized four-poster bed. The bed, welded to a 1,600 cc Volkswagen engine, has insurance, and all legal road-testing, and was inspired by the 1960s TV series The Monkees. "It cost £5,000 and took two months to build," says Edd, "but it impresses the women!" He also drives a bath and a motorized sofa (left).

Hubble, Bubble...

Heavy rains in August 2004 created a bubblefest in Dunn, North Carolina, thanks to soap-based run-off from a factory. A 20-ft (6-m) tall wall of white bubbles obscured the road, but some drivers tried to navigate the mess. Smart ones waited until local firefighters tamed the foam with their hoses.

Put Your Foot in It

A veteran skydiver got his foot caught outside an airplane door and it dangled there in the Pittsburgh skies for 30 minutes. He was still hanging upon landing, but wasn't hurt.

In the Pink

Janette Benson of Macclesfield, England, paid £10,000 ($20,000) to have her Mini Cooper customized— just so that it matched her £20 ($40) handbag! She wanted the new car to be an exact match for her pink bag and splashed out the extra cash for the pink finish and trim.

Home from Home

Charles Miller of Portland, Oregon, created domestic bliss in the back of his truck. The vehicle he made home was 3 ft 9 in (1.2 m) wide and 6 ft (1.8 m) long, and he toured the country clocking up more than 200,000 mi (300,000 km) on the way.

In Distress

After an Oregon man's television began emitting the international distress signal (the 121.5 megahertz beep emitted by crashed airplanes and sinking boats), the Air Force, a county search-and-rescue deputy, and the police arrived at his door. The distress signal had been picked up by a satellite, relayed to an Air-Force base in Virginia, on to the Civil Air Patrol, and finally to officials in Oregon. The man hurried to replace his TV as he didn't want to pay a $10,000 daily fine should his old set pipe up again.

Tough Luck

A 17-year-old teenager from Washington survived a car crash that left her trapped down a ravine in her car for eight days. Doctors think that dehydration may have saved her life, as it stopped a blood clot in her brain from expanding. She was found by an acquaintance, who said she felt led to the site by a dream.

High Jinx

Certain street signs in Eugene, Oregon, routinely get stolen by students attending the University of Oregon as decoration for their rooms. The sign for High Street has been replaced nearly 350 times in the last decade, and the city has spent at least $50,000 on new signs in the last year alone.

Learner Driver

An 11-year-old Kansas City boy, who had previously driven only a tractor, took off on a 200-mi (320-km) trip in the family car after being involved in an argument at his school. At one point he ran out of gas, but some construction workers helped him to refuel. However, his big adventure finally stalled when he locked himself out of the car after taking a break. His parents sent him straight back to school the very next day.

Going Solo

The world's smallest street-legal car was produced on Britain's Isle of Man in the 1960s. The Peel P50 was 53 in (135 cm) high, 53 in (135 cm) long, and 39 in (100 cm) wide. It carried one adult and could reach a top speed of 40 mph (65 km/h).

Close Encounters

In 1996, Nevada State Route 375 was officially named the "Extraterrestrial Highway" by the Nevada Governor, Bob Miller. The highway is, apparently, one of the most "visited" in the country.

Monster Mash

"Bigfoot" is the biggest monster truck in the world: it is 15 ft 5 in (4.7 m) tall, weighs 38,000 lb (17,000 kg) and has 10-ft (3-m) high tires. It was made by Bob Chandler of St. Louis, Missouri.

Drinking and Driving

In 2003, Tony Anchors, from Didcot, England, wanted to do something completely different with his Mini—so he converted it into a mobile bar!

Taking Life To Extremes

Lightning Reactions!

Danielle Stamp, otherwise known as Miss Electra, electrified the audience with her dazzling performance for the Ripley's TV show.

As she sat on a giant tesla coil, 2 million volts of electricity were passed through her and out of her fingertips. To top it all, she didn't feel any pain!

The shocking performance illuminates the audience watching eagerly outside the Ripley's Odditorium in Hollywood, California.

Participants hold up two light strobes at which Miss Electra fires bolts from her fingertips!

The sparks can be seen flowing through the coil and up into the air, passing through Miss Electra.

Coffee Break

The Stella Awards were inspired by Stella Liebeck who, in 1992, spilled a cup of McDonald's coffee onto her lap, burning herself. A New Mexico jury subsequently awarded her $2.9 million in damages. Her name is now used as a label for such U.S. lawsuits.

Ringing the Changes

Cinematographer Ed Lachman, who shot the hit movie *Erin Brockovich*, recently tried a new style of filming: Using Motorola V710 camera phones. He completed five two-minute videos by using six camera phones set at different angles. He projected the six images together, inspired by the works of cubist artists.

Tie Breaker

The world's longest tie—2,300 ft (700 m) long and 82 ft (25 m) wide—has been tied around the Pula Arena, in Croatia. When seagull droppings threatened to ruin the tie, the world's largest owl—a 7-ft (2-m) model—was brought in to guard it.

Food for Thought

Many prestigious art galleries, including the Museum of Modern Art in New York and the Tate Gallery in London, have purchased works of art made by a group of artists called Mondongo. Their pieces are unusual because of the choice of materials used in making them—cheese, cookies, plasticine, cooked meats, and chopsticks are just a few examples!

How the Cookie Crumbles

This portrait is made from cookies on wood by the Mondongo group of artists and was exhibited at the Daniel Maman Fine Art Gallery in Buenos Aires in 2004.

The Veri Thing

A device called the VeriChip, an implantable computer chip to carry medical files, has been approved by the Food and Drug Administration.

The size of a grain of rice, it uses radio frequencies to display a patient's blood type and other medical information when activated by a scanner in a doctor's office.

Playing Away

Joe Cahn, of New Orleans, just hates to miss a single game. Therefore, each fall, for the past nine years, he has hit the road, crisscrossing the U.S.A. to attend both NFL and college football games at more than 50 different stadiums. Cahn estimates that by now he must have racked up nearly 300,000 mi (480,000 km) to appease his habit—and in all those miles, he hasn't received a single traffic ticket. The road is never lonely, he says, as he always travels with Sophie, his pet cat.

The Last Straw

Marco Hort in a recent record-breaking attempt managed to fit 210 drinking straws in his mouth!

A Cold Snap

Audrey Twitchell, of Colorado, made her own skiing outfit from 600 Colorado State sales tax tokens, with a combined value of $1.20.

Eco-logical

A Montana couple have built an environmentally friendly house for less than $15,000. Their cozy abode incorporates 13,000 empty soda and beer cans, and 250 used car tires in its foundation. The savings don't stop there: By heating the house with a wood-burning stove and solar power, the couple's utility bills are only $20 per month.

An Almighty Squash

In 2004, pumpkin-grower Joel Holland produced the winning pumpkin in the 31st annual Safeway World Championship Pumpkin Weigh-off, crushing the chances of 80 other pumpkins to win the prize. Holland had to use a flatbed truck to get his 1,229-lb (557-kg) pumpkin to the competition. To reward his green thumb, Holland received $5 per pound, making his total winnings $6,145.

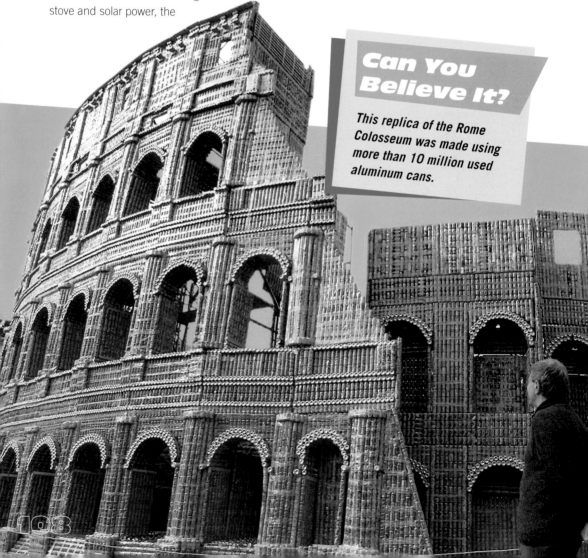

Can You Believe It?

This replica of the Rome Colosseum was made using more than 10 million used aluminum cans.

The Big Picture

Two people were needed to turn one page of this gigantic 16-page book, made by the Mazda car company in 2004. It measured 10 ft (3 m) by 11 ft 3 in (3.5 m), and weighed 776 lb (352 kg).

Jack O' All Lanterns

In 1982, the "king" of giant pumpkins, Howard Dill, of Nova Scotia, Canada, grew the world's largest Jack-o-lantern. It weighed a mighty 445 lb (202 kg) prior to the carving, and measured 10½ ft (3.2 m) in circumference.

THE WORLD'S LARGEST

Steak a Claim

Barcley Prime, an upscale restaurant in Philadelphia, may offer the world's most expensive Philly cheesesteak. Its take on the city favorite, which includes Kobe beef, goose liver, sautéed foie gras, caramelized onions, and shaved truffles, costs $100.

By comparison, typical cheesesteaks, which are usually made with thinly sliced ribeye steak and American cheese, run at around $4.

Catch Your Breath

Shane Shafer, 50, suffered seven months of constant, bark-like hiccups every four seconds before doctors implanted an electronic device in his chest in an innovative operation. All involved breathed long, hiccup-free sighs of relief when Shafer stopped hiccuping.

Watery Grave

A Florida firm offers an unusual resting place for cremated remains: A concrete case on the ocean floor. These "permanent living legacies" are linked to form an artificial commemorative reef in the waters off Palm Beach. Relatives who dive can pay their respects.

Floating Voter

James Pengov, 36, now knows that trying to sell his vote on eBay is illegal. In just 12 hours, authorities heard about—and shut down—Pengov's eBay listing. Pengov, who says he was just trying to pay some medical bills, didn't see the harm in voting for the party favored by his highest bidder, as he was unsure who to vote for.

Take Note

Cops picked up a resident from Pennsylvania for passing counterfeit money: A $200 bill featuring George W. Bush. Clerks at the clothing store didn't realize that the U.S. Mint doesn't actually produce $200 bills. Nor did they notice that it was signed by Ronald Reagan, and that on the back of the bill the White House lawn featured signs saying "We Like Broccoli."

Banana Republic

More than 6 tons of bananas from the Canary Islands were used in the world's first banana pyramid in Madrid, Spain.

Spiral Island

Richie Sowa has created his very own tropical island paradise—out of 250,000 plastic water bottles.

Richie's island home has a large living area, a kitchen, and two bedrooms. The walls are made of plaited palm trees and the roof of plastic sheeting, which also acts as a gutter to collect rainwater for drinking.

The former carpenter from Middlesbrough, England, spent four years constructing Spiral Island, a raft measuring 66 ft (20 m) by 54 ft (16 m) and floating in a lagoon off the exclusive Mexican resort of Puerto Aventuras. He began with a basic raft made from thick bamboo poles, stuffing the bottles, which he obtained from passers-by, into nets tied to the bottom of the poles. The air in the bottles helps to keep the island afloat and he has since planted mangroves, the roots of which grow around the bottles to prevent the man-made island from drifting. The real-life Robinson Crusoe has also nailed layers of plywood on to the poles to provide a solid base for his impressive house, which boasts two bedrooms, a kitchen, and a large living area with walls of plaited palm trees. The roof is covered with plastic sheeting, which collects rainwater for drinking. The mangroves that have been planted help to keep the island cool, and some of them now rise to 15 ft (5 m) high.

The 49-year-old English carpenter had thought about building his own island for a long time, and finally took the plunge just south of Cancun in Mexico.

The Smallest Largest

This traveling museum is one of a kind!

The World's Largest Collection of the World's Smallest Versions of the World's Largest Things museum is situated in none other than a converted Ford Econoline bus!

The World's Largest Collection of the World's Smallest Versions of the World's Largest Things is a display of miniature replicas of oversized sculptures found across the U.S.A. by founder and curator Erika Nelson. She photographs the many giant objects she passes, and collects information about the sculptures. Then she makes and displays a miniature replica along with the information in her museum!

BULL TALKING COW OTTER

TUNE IN
103.1 FM
RADIO

EST VERSIONS WORLDS LARGEST THINGS

ST COLLECTION

www.WORLDSLARGESTTHINGS.com

Festive Farewell

Ozella McHargue, from St. John, Indiana, adored Christmas, so when she died in 2004, her family gave her a Christmas-themed funeral. Even though Ozella died in September, her family decorated the funeral parlor with holly, mistletoe, and a Christmas tree, and instead of somber, funereal music, mourners listened to festive classics such as "Rudolph the Red-Nosed Reindeer."

Blowing Hot and Cold

Known as "the fire-proof man," Singlee was a performer at the Ripley Odditorium in Chicago in the 1930s. He is shown here putting a blow torch to his bare skin, including his eyes.

Domino Effect

A Chinese woman, Ma Lihua, sent the world domino-toppling record crashing in 2003. She took seven weeks to line up 303,628 dominoes (stretching for 9⅓ mi or 15 km) and they came tumbling down in just four minutes. The only threat to her record attempt had come from a stray cockroach, which, during the painstaking preparation, had managed to knock over 10,000 tiles.

Love and Death

A Canadian couple were married in a funeral chapel in 2001. Shane Neufeld and Christy McKillop chose the unconventional venue in Winnipeg, Manitoba, not only because he worked there, but also because it was where they met.

Body Snatchers

Two desperate thieves stole a hearse from outside a Philadelphia church just as it was waiting to take a corpse to a cemetery. Fortunately the corpse wasn't in the vehicle at the time.

Hide and Go Seek

Author Michael Stadther gives treasure-seekers a challenge in his new book *A Treasure's Trove*. In it are clues to where he's hidden 12 tokens that can be redeemed for real jewels. It took eight years to find good hiding places in public areas across the U.S.A.

Jump Ship

Stuntman Robbie Knievel, son of Evel Knievel, jumped seven military aircraft on the deck of an aircraft-carrier in a stunt to promote the launch of a movie about his daredevil father.

Dead Man Talking

Mourners at a chapel of rest in Belgium were horrified when a mobile phone rang inside a coffin. The undertaker had forgotten to take it out of the deceased's clothing.

Shark Meat

British property developer Robert Blackwood wants to be fed to Great White sharks when he dies. His bizarre request was inspired by a TV documentary on the sharks.

Dead Heat

Spiritualist Emma Crawford was buried in 1890 on Red Mountain, near Manitou Springs in Colorado. A landslide in the 1920s suddenly sent her coffin hurtling down into Manitou. Each Halloween the event is commemorated in the Emma Crawford Coffin Races, in which competitors dash along the streets of Manitou carrying coffins containing live Emma look-alikes.

Rainbow Warriors

About 31,000 Filipino students from the Polytechnic University of the Philippines gathered in Manila to form the world's largest human rainbow in 2004.

Million Volt Man

Flickers of ionized krypton, xenon, argon, and neon lightning dance around inside a globe, attracted to the touch of Dean Ortner, the Million Volt Man.

It's Electrifying!

Dr. Dean Ortner used to perform brain surgery on mosquitoes in his former role as a research scientist. Now he's left his lab coat behind to go on the stage, but he still demonstrates his love of science in his *Wonders of Science* programs. His trademark is "riding the lightning," in which he passes a million volts of higher frequency electricity through his body. The power generated makes a board burst into flames, and sends bolts of blue lightning shooting from the fingers of his other hand. He has performed this feat once a week for 30 years, yet he says he's suffered little more than a few burns on his fingertips. The higher frequency doesn't interfere with his nervous system, yet there is still enough power to ignite the wood.

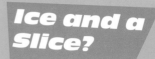

Ice and a Slice?

With a room temperature of -5°C (23°F), the Absolut Icebar in Milan, Italy, has to be one of the coolest places to spend an evening!

Turkish Delight

Thousands of Turks helped to carry the world's longest national flag through the center of Istanbul in 2003. At 2½ mi (4 km) long, the flag was created to mark the 80th anniversary of the foundation of the Turkish Republic.

Smoke Signal

A Romanian smoker made a coffin out of more than 7,000 cigarette packs in 2001. Mihai Cepleuca said he wanted to be buried in it to show that smoking really can put people into their graves.

Worm's Eye View

His body wrapped in saran wrap, Welsh performance artist Paul Hurley spent nine days slithering around a field in 2004 to see what life is like as an earthworm. He spent his time burrowing, pausing only to eat a leaf or grain of soil. He saw this as "an exploration of the earth and dirtiness." He has previously coated himself in jelly to become a slug, and dressed as a snail and licked the inside of a greenhouse for two hours.

Pay Your Respects

A man from Schopfheim, Germany, was so keen to save on funeral costs that he tied his dead mother's coffin to his roof rack and drove her along the motorway to the cemetery.

Off-color

In Georgia, a company called Collegiate Memorials allows college football fans to go to their graves proudly displaying their loyalty. The company makes special caskets and urns emblazoned with a university's colors.

DEAD END
BEE LN

No Ordinary Joe

Mastocytosis is an incurable disease that affects approximately one person in every 500,000. Joe Tornatore is one such person: He experiences anaphylactic shock whenever a foreign substance, such as the venom from a bee sting, enters his body. While participating in a two-year immunotherapy program, Joe wore a beekeeper's suit to protect himself every single time he went outdoors.

The Farmer Wants a Wife

An Ohio man paid a farmer to carve the words, "Michelle, will you marry me?" into his corn crop. The bride-to-be melted into giggles—and said "Yes"—when she spied the message from a small plane.

Buried Alive

A 50-year-old Czech man, Zdenek Zahradka, claimed a new world record in June 2004 by surviving for ten days buried underground in a wooden coffin without food or water. He lost 19 lb (9 kg) in weight during his ordeal and said he spent most of his incarceration sleeping.

Round the Clock

Jay Larson, founder of the International Speed Golf Association, shot a 72 on a 6,500-yd (5,945-m) course near San Diego, California, in just 39 minutes 55 seconds, averaging less than two-and-a-half minutes per hole. Under the association's rules, the number of strokes is added to the time to calculate the player's score—in Larson's case, 111.55.

All Hands on Deck

Christina Shaw exhibits a 16 ft (5 m) deckchair sculpture at the Three Counties Show held in Worcestershire, England.

In the Swim

Environmental activist Christopher Swain, of Portland, Oregon, jumps right in if needed. His latest feat was swimming the 80 mi (130 km) of the Charles River, in Massachusetts, to ensure the Environmental Protection Agency keeps to its goal of making it swimmable by 2005. Parts of the river are badly polluted with sewage, trash, and pesticides.

Cookie Monster

A giant chocolate-chip cookie, baked by the Immaculate Baking Company in 2003, weighed in at a staggering 40,000 lb (18,150 kg). Displayed at Flat Rock, North Carolina, it took eight hours to bake, and required 30,000 eggs and a cookie sheet the size of a basketball court!

Have Your Cake and Eat It

In 2004, Serbian baker Zvonko Mihajlovic unveiled what he claimed was the world's biggest birthday cake. Thousands of residents of Nis tucked into the 400-ft (122-m) long cake, which weighed more than two tons and was made using 2,100 eggs and 1,500 lb (680 kg) of sugar.

Big Cheese

A South African hypermarket made a pizza 122 ft 8 in (37.4 m) in diameter, using 9,920 lb (4,500 kg) of flour, 1,984 lb (900 kg) of tomato purée, 1,984 lb (900 kg) of tomatoes, 3,968 lb (1,800 kg) of cheese, and 1,763 lb (800 kg) of mushrooms. It took 39 hours to prepare and cook.

Holy Smoke!

It took New Yorker, Vincent Pennisi, seven years to create this 38-in (97-cm) high wooden model of Milan's cathedral.

Bouncing Back

In 1999, David Kirke, of the Dangerous Sports Club, celebrated the 21st anniversary of the first ever bungee jump by repeating the leap off the Clifton Suspension Bridge in Bristol, England.

High Flying

As if walking along a beam from one hot-air balloon to another at 4,000 ft (1,220 m) wasn't daring enough, pilot Mike Howard complicated his feat by wearing a blindfold!

The two hot-air balloons had been tied together in the skies over Bristol, England, to prevent them from drifting apart. It took Mike a nerve-wracking three minutes to walk the 19-ft (6-m) beam. He then parachuted to the ground to meet his wife and daughter.

Madhatters' Tea Party

In 2001, stuntmen Julian Saunders, Rob Oliver, and Ross Taylor became the first people to take tea atop a hot-air balloon. After having tea at 4,920 ft (1,500 m) over Melbourne, Australia, they abseiled down the side of the balloon back into the basket.

Armchair Traveler

Balloon pilot Pete Dalby floated above Bristol, England, in the comfort of his own armchair, which had been strapped to a specially adapted hot-air balloon.

SWEB
ENERGY

Pushing the Envelope

When Jeff Datwyler picked up a stray envelope off an Ohio street in 2004, he assumed it was trash. When he opened it, he found a check for $15,000. The irony is that, across town, the person who had lost the envelope was standing in a bank line, blissfully unaware that he'd lost his deposit. Just as he was reaching into his pocket for the check, his bank notified him that it had been found.

Short Circuit

The World's Shortest St. Patrick's Day parade took place on March 17, 2004, in the town of Hot Springs, Arkansas. The town staged its parade on Bridge Street, the thoroughfare which, at a quarter the length of a normal city block, has a claim to being the shortest street in the world.

Brought to Book

New York student Steve Stanzak spent seven months sleeping in his university's library because he could not afford accommodation costs. He was finally discovered in April 2004.

A Rise in Inflation

Manoj Chopra, of India, inflated a hot-water bottle at the World Strongman Cup to display the extraordinary power of his lungs.

Banana George

George Blair learned to snowboard at 75, drove a racing car for the first time at 81, made his first parachute jump at 82, and took bull-riding lessons at 85!

Age has never been a barrier for the 90-year-old extreme sports fanatic—he made just as much of a splash in 2004, when he was pulled along Florida's Lake Florence at 40 mph (65 km/h), as when he went waterskiing barefoot in icy Antarctica when he was a youthful 71. George's favorite fruit is the banana, and most of his possessions are yellow, even his sunglasses and phone— hence his nickname, "Banana George." In 2002, *Sports Illustrated for Women* put George in the magazine's annual swimsuit issue. "I had never thought of myself as one of the world's sexiest men," he admitted. "But I like it."

George is known to everyone as "Banana George" because of his love of all things yellow. He wears yellow clothes, drives a yellow car, and bounces across the lake behind a yellow speedboat.

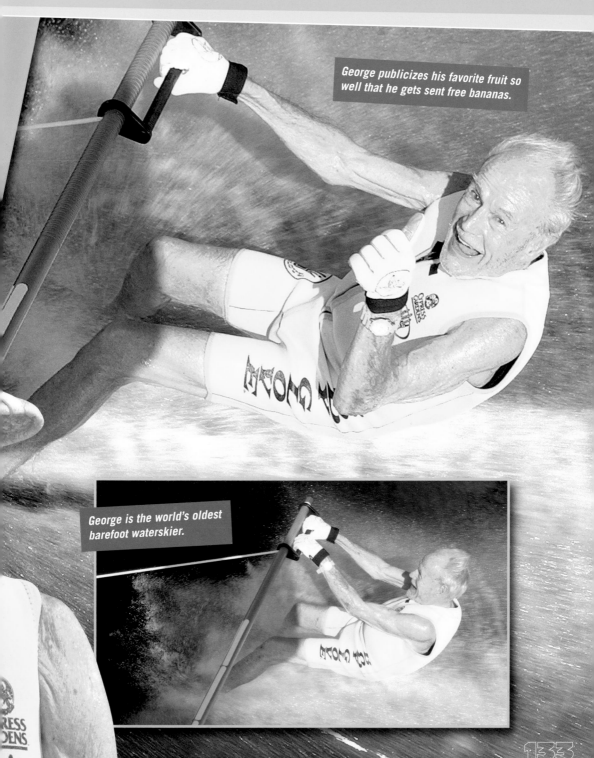

George publicizes his favorite fruit so well that he gets sent free bananas.

George is the world's oldest barefoot waterskier.

A Tight Squeeze

In 2003, 14 people from the Kabosh theater group from Belfast, Northern Ireland, squeezed into a phone booth in Edinburgh, Scotland, to break the world record by two people. One said: "It was pretty claustrophobic in there, but it's a quick way to get to know people!"

Pillow Talk

No fewer than 645 people took part in a mass pillow fight in the town square at Gannet, Kansas, in June 2003.

Heavy Reading

Michael Hawley, a scientist at the Massachusetts Institute of Technology, has written the world's largest published book—a 133-lb (60-kg) tome entitled *Bhutan: A Virtual Odyssey Across the Kingdom*. Measuring 5 ft (1.5 m) by 7 ft (2.1 m), it used 1 gal (4.5 l) of ink and enough paper to cover a football field. The author admitted: "It's not a book to curl up with at bedtime— unless you plan to sleep on it!"

Tip of the Iceberg

Entitled "The Ice Cube Project," this red iceberg floating in Ilulissat Fiord in Greenland, was created in two hours by artist Marco Evaristti, using 6,340 pt (3,000 l) of paint, seawater, three fire hoses, two ice-breakers, and 20 men.

Pole Star

A former pilot with the Royal Canadian Air Force, Jack Mackenzie joined a nine-member ski expedition to the North Pole in 1999… at the age of 77! To reach the Pole, the sprightly septuagenarian had to ski for up to seven hours a day.

Layer Cake

In 1953, Primo Maca, of California, baked this 15½ ft (5 m) tall giant cake, which fed a total of 10,500 people!

Be Dazzled!

At £15,250 ($30,500), Dazzle is surely the world's most expensive cocktail! A concoction of rosé champagne, strawberry liquor, lychee liquor, lemon juice, and syrup, topped with a white gold and diamond ring, it certainly dazzled diners at the Bar & Brasserie of Harvey Nichols department store in Manchester, England.

Flower Power

Melvin A. Hemker, 82, of St. Charles, Michigan, grew a sunflower in 2001 that had 837 heads and was so heavy that it needed three wooden braces for support. The previous record for a sunflower was a mere 129 heads.

The Pony Express

Indian policeman Sailendra Nath Roy pulled a bus by his ponytail for 100 ft (30 m) in 2003. Previously, he had pulled a van and a jeep with his ponytail and lifted a 45 lb (20 kg) weight with his mustache.

Global Village

In 2001, 13,588 "Village People" danced to the song "YMCA" before a baseball game in Omaha, Nebraska.

Watt a Bargain

A 40-watt bulb in Fort Worth, Texas, has been burning non-stop for nearly a century! The bulb, which cost just a few cents, was originally fitted above the backstage door at the Palace Theater on September 21, 1908, with orders that it was never to be switched off. Still going strong, it now lights up the Stockyards Museum.

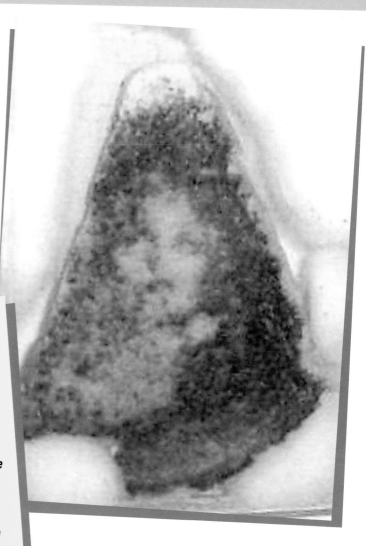

Raise a Toast

A half-eaten grilled cheese sandwich sold on eBay for a whopping £15,000 ($30,000). Diana Duyser put the toastie up for sale on the Internet auction site because she was staggered by the likeness of the Virgin Mary that the sandwich bore. The page was viewed more than 100,000 times before the auction ended.

Binocular Vision

Frank Gehry designed this spectacular binocular-shaped building in Venice, Los Angeles.

Gift of the Gab

To celebrate the start of her 19th season on U.S. television, talkshow host Oprah Winfrey gave every one of her 276-strong studio audience a brand new $25,000 car.

Man Bites Dog

A 23-year-old man from Bend, Oregon, suspected of assaulting his girlfriend, bit a police dog on the head as he tried to avoid arrest. The dog, named Amor, had just bitten the suspect on the leg.

Pushing His Luck

A man was arrested in Blue Lake, California, in 2004 after police officers saw him doing one-handed push-ups in the middle of the State Highway 299. He was trying to get a lift home and thought his daring fitness routine would force a driver to stop for him!

Wind Bag

Solicitor's clerk Paul Hunn, from London, England, trains on an unusual diet of carbonated drinks and spicy foods. Why? He is the world's loudest burper! In 2000, Paul belched at 118.1 decibels—as loud as a pneumatic drill.

Reaching His Peak

Salvation Mountain near Niland, California, is America's craziest peak. Made from hay bales and adobe, topped with a giant cross, it is 100 ft (30 m) wide and rises three stories high above the desert. Leonard Knight, a former car mechanic who built the mountain 17 years ago, has defied government attempts to demolish it, and lives at its foot in an old truck without electricity or water.

Butter Nuts

A Swedish couple out hunting in the northern province of Jaemtland were alarmed to stumble across 70 pairs of shoes, all filled with butter. Sneakers, stilettos, and boots were all stuffed with 1 lb (0.5 kg) of butter and spread out over the landscape.

Baby Bell

Steve Hough is the proud owner of the world's smallest working bell-tower, which he built in his back garden in Gosport, England. Named "Little Ben" it's a tribute to its larger namesake, London's Big Ben.

Super Sculptures

The U.S.A. is home to a spectacular range of oversized sculptures.

Minnesota is littered with such attractions, and one of them is a 33-ft (10-m) tall statue of the legendary lumberjack Paul Bunyan (opposite), in front of the Paul Bunyan Historical Society Museum in Akeley.

High Point, North Carolina, the self-proclaimed "Home Furnishing Capital of the World," boasts a 33-ft (10-m) chest of drawers. The attraction has stood there since the Chamber of Commerce built it in 1926.

The 12-ft (4-m) prairie dog statue in Interior, South Dakota, stands guard outside The Ranch Store souvenir stand. Not only can you see the world's largest prairie dog statue here, but you can also feed or even buy real prairie dogs.

HA SCHULT
LOVELETTERS
BUILDING
EIN BRIEF SETZT ZEICHEN

Am 3. Juli 2001 rief HA Schult alle
Freunde und Kunden der Deutschen Post
auf, einen Liebesbrief zu schreiben, an
wen oder was auch immer und damit
einen Baustein zu liefern für die größte
Liebes-Skulptur der Welt.
In sechsmonatiger Arbeit entstand aus
mehr als 150.000 Liebesbriefen ein
Denkmal der Gefühle im Herzen Berlin
Die Liebe ist die einzige Kraft gegen de
Krieg.

Maße der Skulptur:
Länge Oranienburger Straße 54 Meter
Länge Tucholskystraße 88 Meter
Eingangsanlage 10 Meter
Höhe der Kuppel 39 Meter

Anzahl der Briefe am Gebäude: 35.000
Anzahl der Briefe im Gebäude: ca. 115.000

Aufbauzeit:
13. August bis 11. Oktober 2001
Anzahl der Mitarbeiter: 50

Stamp of Approval

The German Post Office
in Berlin promoted their
building by covering
all 130,000 sq ft
(12,000 sq m) of it with
thousands of love letters.

Taking the Plunge

A Canadian prankster plunged into the pool during the men's diving competition at the 2004 Athens Olympics wearing a tutu and tights!

Leap of Faith

Fitted with artificial knees and a hearing-aid, 92-year-old Herb Tanner completed his first parachute jump in 1998 when he leaped from a plane 3,500 ft (1,067 m) above Cleveland, Ohio. A pilot for 63 years, Herb had always wanted to make a parachute jump, but his wife had threatened to leave him if he ever did so. When she died in 1996, he was finally able to make his dream come true.

Dead Ringers

The funeral of Dane Squires was interrupted in 2004 when the deceased phoned his family to say he wasn't dead! His sister had identified him as the victim of a railroad accident in Toronto, Ontario, but the burial was put on hold when Dane called to say that the mutilated body was someone else's.

Get the Message?

Mexican Laura Carmona made her message loud and clear to boyfriend Alfonso Hernandez when she covered his car in love letters on St. Valentine's Day!

Animal Antics

Worm His Way Out

Buried up to his chin in more than 10,000 earthworms, Mark Hogg wormed his way out by actually eating some of them!

Survivalist Mark was gradually buried in the earthworms, then proceeded to eat them—without using his hands—for a whole hour.

That's a whole lot of worms!

Two Ripley employees started to load up the container around Mark.

Keep 'em coming.

Once buried, he was watched by eager spectators as he started to eat.

147

Chipmunk Cheek

When Charlie the chipmunk decided he was thirsty, a long, cool glass of freshly squeezed orange juice didn't last very long. Charlie deftly sucks on the straw before diving head-first into the glass and gulping the lot!

High Steaks

When Romanian health officials investigated a strange smell coming from the home of Gyenge Lajos, they discovered that the 74-year-old was storing a dead cow in his living room! Apparently he had been given the animal by a friend and carved and cooked strips of the rotting corpse when he felt hungry.

This Bone's Chewy

If your dog's breath is causing offense, you need to give your pooch chewing gum for dogs. The gum, which is made by the Brazilian company Chiclet, looks like a bone and is made from edible leather.

Oh Deer

You might be surprised to learn that the most dangerous animals at large in the U.S.A. are not bears, sharks, poisonous snakes, or even spiders—but deer. The mild-mannered mammals are responsible for the deaths of about 100 people every year because they often cause road accidents. Bees, dogs, rattlesnakes, and spiders also rank among the top five killers of the animal world.

Best-dressed Crab

First held in 1975, the Miss Crustacean Hermit-crab Beauty Contest draws hundreds of enthusiasts to the beach at Ocean City, New Jersey, for the search to find the best-dressed crab. Past entries have included Cleopatra Crab and Crabzilla.

Monkey Business

Declaring that he wanted to be "at one with the monkeys," 32-year-old Peter Vetique stripped down to his boxer shorts, scaled a 20-ft (6-m) high fence and jumped into the gorilla enclosure at New York's Bronx Zoo in 2001.

Lounge Lizards

In 2002, police called to a man's apartment in Newark, Delaware, after he had failed to report for work, found his body on the floor… and his pet Nile monitor lizards feeding on his flesh.

Feline Romantic

In 1996, two very rare "diamond-eyed" cats called Phet and Ploy were married in a Thai disco. The event cost $16,241.

On the Couch

Pam Whyte, a canine therapist from Cape Town, South Africa, has a consultation with a collie.

Holy Cow!

Cats, dogs, gerbils, guinea pigs, parakeets, and a tortoise were among the congregation at the 2003 Blessing of the Animals' service at Saint Philip's in the Hills Episcopal Church, Tucson, Arizona. Hundreds of owners and their pets gathered for the service, which went off peacefully apart from a Beagle barking during prayers.

Meowing Muse

When Marilyn, a Doberman Pinscher, ran away from her new home in Sault Ste Marie, Ontario, in 2002, owners Ron and Peggy Lund lured her back using a borrowed kitten. The dog adores kittens and was powerless to resist the plaintive miaowing.

Like Headless Chickens

Commemorating a story about a chicken from the 1940s that allegedly lived for 18 months

Dog Spa

A hot spring in Tokyo, Japan, has shelled out on a new annex—designed especially for dogs! For as little as $25, pets can enjoy a hot tub filled with volcanic waters, before retiring to a luxury room for a dog nap.

after having its head chopped off, the town of Fruita, Colorado, holds an annual "Mike the Headless Chicken Day." Events include the 3 mi (4.8 km) "Run Like a Headless Chicken Race," egg tosses, "Pin the Head on the Chicken," "Chicken Bingo," and the classic "Chicken Dance."

The Price of Luxury

Some of the priciest pets coveted by Americans cost more than a luxury car. For example, a lavender albino ball python will set you back approximately $40,000, a striped ball python will cost you $20,000, and a reticulated albino tiger python costs a wopping $15,000.

Suite Talk

A pet hotel in Fairfax County, Virginia, charges $230 for a dog's use of a hydrotherapy pool, state-of-the-art exercise room, beauty parlor, and suites with satellite TV and classical music.

Gator Aid

Matthew Goff didn't hesitate to stab a 6-ft (1.8-m) alligator in the eye with his pocket knife after it attempted to nab his puppy, Sugar. When she was off her leash, Sugar wandered to the edge of the pond, and the alligator took the opportunity to grab her head. Fortunately for 29-year-old Matthew, jabbing the reptile in its eye was the right move. Sugar managed to scamper home, with only three teeth marks to show for her near-death experience.

Snake in the Grass

A New Jersey man tried to steal two pythons and was bitten for his actions. The 20-year-old thief managed to slip the snakes out of a pet store in canvas bags attached to his pants. But on the drive home one of the snakes wrapped around the man's leg and latched on to his groin.

The Hitcher

A Russian Blue/Angora cross-bred cat by the name of Tracker went on an unplanned 150-mi (241-km) ride from Kalamazoo to Rochester Hills, Michigan, when Patricia Verduin, a college student, drove home for Christmas. Despite traveling under the hood, Tracker didn't seem harmed by the experience.

To Dye For...

Coloring your hair is no longer the preserve of humans. A pet grooming parlour in Chongqing, China, has started to offer services for pets including haircut and color.

Fir Goodness' Sake

For some reason, a dog in Denver, Colorado, scampered 30 ft (9 m) up a blue spruce tree. Amused city workers had to enlist the services of a cherry-picker to bring the poor pooch down to earth.

The Great Escape

Red is one cunning dog, but kennel owners hope his jail breaks are a thing of the past. Red's expertise, it seems, is breaking out of his cage at Battersea Dogs' Home, London, England, for midnight raids on the kitchen—and freeing the other dogs to join him. Having observed Red's technique on video, staff have added extra security devices to his kennel.

More Than You Can Chew

A 50-lb (23-kg) flathead catfish had to be rescued after it playfully grabbed a basketball—and got it stuck in its mouth!

The catfish wrapped its jaws around the basketball, which was floating in the water, but the ball got stuck in the fish's tight grip. Pam and Bill Driver, from Wichita, Kansas, saw that the fish was in trouble and could not swim freely with the ball wedged in its mouth, and they began a brave rescue attempt.

It becomes clear to the Drivers that the catfish is in need of help, so Bill goes to the aid of the fish and gets into the water.

The ball is jammed so tightly into the catfish's mouth that it's a struggle to remove it—but it has to be done to allow the fish to swim freely again.

Bill finally manages to get hold of the catfish and pull the basketball from its tight grip.

Sonic Saviors

Dr. Michael Hyson, dolphin researcher, says that dolphins can generate sound and electromagnetic fields that may be able to help treat human diseases. He believes they have something to contribute in the treatment of conditions such as autism, cerebral palsy, and depression. Speaking from experience, he says that a dolphin helped to heal a couple of painful dislocated vertebrae in his own back when he went swimming with the creature.

Party Animal

In 2004, British pet-lover Jan Einzig threw a champagne party at a top London club for her West Highland terrier Gucci. To date, she has also spent more than £12,000 ($23,000) on vet's bills for treatments for the ailing dog.

Insect-lover

A lonely widower in Beijing, China, kept some 200,000 cockroaches in his home as pets. He began breeding them following the death of his wife.

Flight of Fancy

American entrepreneurs Mark and Lorraine Moore have been raking in big bucks by selling bird diapers through their company, the appropriately titled Avian Fashions. The Lycra suits, which cost between $20 and $26, allow pet birds to roam freely around their owner's house without soiling the furniture—that is as long as the pads are changed every six hours. The Moores say that their friends and family initially thought the idea was rather "flighty."

Crocodile Priority

Patients waiting for ultrasound treatment at a hospital in Croatia were kept waiting for hours after a doctor took his 4-ft (1.2-m) pet crocodile for a check-up.

Milking it

This huge 1928 statue commemorates the world's champion milk-producing cow—it produced an amazing 3,739 gal (16,997 l) of milk in one of its record-beating years! It also produced 2,865 lb (1,300 kg) of butter. You can see just how many milk bottles would have been needed to contain all the milk.

HERE LIVED
AND GAVE HER SERVICE TO MANKIND
SEGIS·PIETERTJE PROSPECT
WORLD'S CHAMPION MILK COW
BORN 1913   DIED 1925

Cat People

A Georgia couple adopted 77 cats, with the Humane Society's blessing, because they take such good care of them. All of the felines are healthy, well fed, and given access to lots and lots of litter boxes. The couple go through 60 lb (27 kg) of cat litter each week.

Fat Chance

Pumpkin, who weighed 12 lb (5 kg), was certainly one chubby Chihuahua. Her Florida owner took her to the local veterinary surgeon for a little liposuction, where they removed 12 oz (340 g) of fat.

However, the surgeon reminded Pumpkin's owner that in order to stay svelte, the pooch really needed to take regular exercise and wolf down fewer treats.

Café Society

The Meow Mix Café opened on Fifth Avenue in New York City in 2004. The cat clientele are offered various different Meow Mix varieties. Alternatives to cat food are available for their owners.

Champion Chimp

Animals can be just as creative us humans. You only have to look at the works of art produced by Asuka, a three-year-old chimpanzee, who made her debut in the art world when she exhibited 50 of her paintings in Tokyo in 2004.

Do You Take Amex?

Her Highness Princess Zarina Zainal of Malaysia thinks nothing of traveling halfway around the globe to visit the vet with her 16-year-old Yorkshire terrier, Amex. Every trip involves a 14-hour flight from Bangkok to Paris, followed by a seven-hour flight from Paris to New York, and then a two-hour drive to the vet's office in the town of South Salem, New York state.

Playful Pigs

Pigs were taught to play video games and hit targets and match objects, using their snouts to control the joysticks. The feat was set-up and recorded by Prof. Curtis at Pennsylvania State University. Rewards came in the form of candies.

Ear, Ear

Jack, a two-year-old Basset Hound, has ears that measure a whopping 13 in (33 cm) in length! Jack's ears are insured for $50,000.

It's a Dog's Life

You may think that luxury is the sole preserve of humankind, but you'd be wrong.

Now your pets can be treated to exactly the same kind of pampering as you. You can even treat them to such delights as a night in a top-quality hotel, at which they can experience a hot-spring treatment!

A hotel in Paris, France, has taken customer service to the next level. The hotel staff are all specially trained to deliver the highest-quality food and service to pets!

Four Paw-ster

Who couldn't get a good night's sleep in a luxury four-poster bed? Evie was a lucky enough dog to spend the night in one of designer Jane Evans' luxurious bespoke doggy beds.

Bark-itecture

This state-of-the-art dog kennel, designed by architect Lisa Vogt, sold for $9,200 when it was auctioned for charity in Florida in 2004.

Honey Bunch
Steve Conlon runs a honey business in West Virginia. The honey-bees join in Steve's unusual party piece: Wearing a living "beard" of about 10,000 bees on his face!

Trick or Treat?
Michele Carlin of Michigan sells Halloween costumes for dogs from her store, the Puppy Boutique. She takes her own Yorkshire terrier and Schnauzer trick-or-treating, and encourages others to do the same.

The Importance of Being Ernest's
About 60 cats live at the Ernest Hemingway Home and Museum in Key West, Florida. Most are descended from Hemingway's pet cat, Princess Six Toes.

All the Presidents' Pets
The Presidential Pet Museum in Maryland, just 20 mi (30 km) from the White House, has more than 500 items related to the pets of past presidents.

Doggy-vision

German police who were responding to a complaint about excessively loud noise had to force their way into a house when no one answered the door. They were surprised to find Bruno the Alsatian cross-breed sitting on the couch with his paw on the television's remote control.

Sign Here, Please

Rin Tin Tin, a German Shepherd, was Hollywood's first canine star. He starred in 27 movies, always signing his contracts with paw prints. His death in 1932 made front-page news.

Packing a Punch

George W. Bush's pet Scottish Terrier appeared in a spoof political video during the campaign trail for the 2004 election. Barney the dog was shown dressed in a headband and barking at Jon Kerry's dog, with the theme from the Rocky films playing as background music.

Bear-faced Cheek

Juan, an Andean spectacled bear, made a dramatic bid for freedom at Germany's Berlin Zoo in August 2004. First he paddled across a moat using a log as a raft, then he scaled the wall of his enclosure. Bizarrely, he looked to complete his getaway on a bicycle, which he found standing against the zoo railings. However, before he could climb onto the saddle, he was cornered by zoo-keepers wielding brooms, and immobilized with a tranquilizer dart.

Giddy Up

Whiplash the monkey is a rodeo act with a difference—he rode in a tiny saddle on the back of a Collie to herd sheep at the annual Calgary Stampede in Alberta, Canada.

163

On the Double

This piglet, born in China in 2002, had two heads and three eyes.

Ready Meal

"Buck" Fulford claimed an astonishing feat by killing, plucking, cooking, and eating a chicken in 1 minute 50 seconds. His method? He held the chicken upside-down and cut off its head, allowing 40 seconds for it to die, 10 seconds for scalding, 5 seconds to remove feathers, cut out its entrails, and cut it into four portions, dropped it into boiling fat for 30 seconds, then placed it in cracked ice for a further 25 seconds!

When it Comes to the Crunch

In a divorce settlement in Edmonton, Canada, Kenneth Duncan was ordered to pay his ex-wife $200 every month in dog support. On top of that, he also had to dig deep to fund a $2,000 retroactive payment for the care of their St. Bernard, Crunchy.

Silver Service

English eccentric Francis Henry Egerton, the eighth Earl of Bridgwater, had 12 dogs that ate with him every day at formal dinners. The dogs were served from silver dishes.

Parrot Fashion

A Congo African Gray parrot called N'Kisi, owned by Aimee Morgana of Manhattan, has astonished the scientific world with its vocabulary of more than 700 words. It has also impressed others with its accurate use of tenses of verbs, its keen sense of humor, and even its amazing telepathic abilities.

Take a Pew

The St. Francis Episcopal Church in Stamford, Connecticut, provides special church services, and even Holy Communion, for pets.

Emergency Service

Firefighters in Florida have oxygen masks to help anyone who might have inhaled smoke… including pets. They carry masks for cats, dogs, and even hamsters.

Married to the Mutt

A nine-year-old Indian girl, Karnamoni Handsa, married a dog in order to ward off an evil omen. Village elders said she would be free to marry a man when she was older, and wouldn't need a divorce from the dog.

Piggy in the Middle

A Bengal tiger called Saimai was suckled by a sow and grew up with a litter of piglets. The unusual family lives peacefully at the Si Racha tiger farm in Thailand.

Pump Up the Volume

Serbian farmers have found a secret weapon to help deter the wild boars that destroy their crops: Loud rock music. People play it at full volume to scare away their porcine visitors—apparently Meatloaf has proven especially effective.

Unscheduled Departure

Billy the cat was put on to a flight from Phoenix, Arizona, bound for Philadelphia, where he was due to transfer to a connecting international flight. Billy somehow managed to escape from his cage and ended up stuck in the plane's cargo hold for 19 days. Eventually, the cat was discovered at Manchester Airport in New Hampshire, and finally reunited with his owners.

Dressed Up to the Canines!

The annual ten-day Fantasy Fest held in Key West, Florida, is a chance for everyone to get dressed up and have some fun. It's not just humans who get to join in—pets from across the U.S.A. come to compete in the Pet Masquerade and Parade. Events include the Pet/Owner Look-alike competition, in which owners and pets dress in matching outfits to suit their chosen theme—ranging from historical figures, such as Marie Antoinette, to sports, such as scuba-diving.

Peri Stone and her pet Woody entered in 2002, using The Beatles' "Yellow Submarine" as their theme.

"Miss Trouble," a five-year-old Mexican green iguana, entered the Pet/Owner Look-alike competition in the 2000 Fantasy Fest. Her owner, Todd Heins, took the contest very seriously and did a convincing job of making himself up to resemble his beloved reptile.

167

Making a Splash

Grey squirrels are renowned for their athleticism, but Twiggy can do more than just climb trees. Under the watchful eye of Florida trainer Lou Ann Best, Twiggy demonstrates her skills as a water-skier at boat shows across America. Twiggy is towed around a 6-in (15-cm) deep inflatable pool at speeds of up to 6 mph (10 km/h) by a remote-controlled model boat. Lou Ann says the key to training Twiggy is affection, patience,… and plenty of nuts.

Litter Bugs

The Feline Evolution CatSeat is a toilet seat for cats, which is mounted on a regular toilet. Apparently it takes two to three weeks for a cat to get used to it.

Going the Whole Hog

Anne Langton, of Derbyshire, England, holds the world record for the largest collection of pig-related objects. She owns more than 10,000 porcine knick-knacks, including piggy banks, teapots, kettles, and plush toys.

Only the Best

Pigs, cats, monkeys, and even horses are permitted to fly on U.S. airlines—but only in first class.

Finders, Keepers

A Cincinnati couple paid a $10,000 reward to a man who found their dog after it had gone missing.

Animal Hospital

An injured labrador made its own way to Beckley Appalachian Regional Hospital in West Virginia after it had been hit by a car.

The Downward Dog

A chain of gyms in the U.S.A. offers yoga classes specially designed for dogs and their owners, claiming that the exercise reduces the levels of canine stress.

Speeding Bill

In 2002, a traffic radar camera in northern Germany caught a speeding... duck. The bird must have been flying fast to set off the radar system, but a precise speed could not be determined.

169

Two Heads are Better than One

Trixie, a blue-tongued lizard with two heads, was discovered in Australia.

Cool Mules

Mule Day, a four-day celebration of the humble mule, is held every year in Columbia, Tennessee. Thousands of visitors come from far and wide to attend the festivities, which include mule shows, arts and crafts booths, and a parade.

Speed Limit

The peregrine falcon is the world's fastest living creature. The birds can reach speeds of between 124 mph (200 km/h) and 168 mph (270 km/h) when swooping from great heights or while catching birds in mid-air.

Paws for Thought

Most cats have five toes on each paw, but Robert Ripley documented many cases of multi-toed cats. One, Whitney, who lived with his owner in New York, had as many as 32 toes—eight on each paw!

Switched On

Monique Cadonic thinks that her male cat, Lincoln, a Russian Blue cross, might just be trying to communicate something. Lincoln appears to take great pleasure in batting light switches on and off— particularly when Monique's husband has just got into the shower.

Shaggy Sheep Story

Shrek, a runaway merino ram who was loose for six years in New Zealand, was finally caught by shepherds after surviving several harsh winters. His huge fleece was so overgrown that it weighed 60 lb (27 kg). He was finally shorn by former blade-shearing world champion Peter Casserly— in a speedy 20 minutes! Shrek's mammoth fleece was later auctioned for a children's charity.

One of the Family

Maddy, a three-year-old chocolate Labrador Retriever, knows just how much her owner loves her because, without the slightest hesitation, he gave her mouth-to-mouth resuscitation. When Maddy got into difficulties in a river, her owner dived in to save her. He then compressed her chest and blew air into her mouth as he performed CPR. He says that's just what you do for family members.

Law and Order

The black squirrels of Council Bluffs, Iowa, are protected by a law that says that people must not "annoy, worry, maim, injure, or kill" any of them.

Two of a Kind

Scientists in Texas successfully cloned a cat for the first time on December 22, 2001. Rather surprisingly, the aptly named CopyCat owes its existence to a rich dog-lover, Dr. John Sperling, who has poured millions of dollars into research for the Missyplicity Project. The project began as an attempt to clone Sperling's much-loved mongrel dog Missy. Sadly, Missy died in 2002, but gene-banking technology means that her DNA is available for cloning when it becomes possible. So far, cloning a cat has proved simpler than cloning a dog, but research continues. As news of the Missyplicity Project spread, requests came in from people all over the world who wanted to clone their own beloved pets. Although it costs many thousands of dollars, cat cloning is now available—and it is thought that dog cloning will be before too long.

Bark 'n' Boots

Police in Northumbria, England, are issuing their police dogs boots to protect their paws. Police officers think they will prove especially useful in crime scenes where there is glass on the floor.

Slippery Customer

Pulling a snake through your nose and out of your mouth is not everyone's idea of fun, but this man in Madras, India, made a feat of it. He also swallowed 200 worms in 20.22 seconds!

173

I Smell a Cat

The case against a drug suspect in Waterloo, Iowa, was dismissed in 2003 because the police sniffer-dog had failed to complete the search. The highly trained dog had abandoned its duty in order to chase a passing cat.

Doggy Bag

Canadian inventor Paul Le Fevre has come up with a dual-purpose "doggy bag." Although it has a compartment for dog food, it is essentially a designer diaper for dogs so that dog-owners can keep the streets clean.

Dandy Wharhol

Jacqui Adams is the proud owner of the world's fastest ferret, Warhol. At the 1999 North of England Ferret Racing Championships, Warhol sped 32 ft (10 m) in 12.59 seconds.

Ready, Steady, Slow!

At the 2004 World Championship Snail Race, the prize-winning mollusk was Owen, who stole the show with a record time of 2 minutes 10 seconds to reach the finish line of the 13-in (33-cm) course. Snails secrete mucus from a special gland that enables them to slide on one foot, and they can apparently reach speeds of between 0.029 and 0.0063 mph (0.013 and 0.0028 m/sec).

Cub Love

When Cora the tiger cub was born in a circus in France, her mother didn't have enough milk to feed her. So she was adopted by a kindly Pointer called Diane.

Unusual Upbringing

A seven-year-old boy was raised by a dog in a remote part of Siberia after being abandoned by his parents at the age of three months. When he was found in August 2004 he couldn't talk and had canine traits like walking on all fours and growling.

Startling Starlings

No one knows why 300 dead starlings dropped out of the sky in Tacoma, Washington, in 1998. One theory suggests that they were blown to the ground by a violent gust of strong wind.

175

A Feather in her Cap

In 1947, Beverly Bell spent five hours creating this dress made entirely from turkey feathers. It's not just the dress that is made from feathers, the shoes are also made from quill ends.

Asking for Trouble

Trouble, a six-year-old beagle, recently set his paw prints in concrete when he was honored with a place in the Canine World Heroes Walk of Fame. Trouble is a star in the canine world, because he managed to sniff out 1.3 million lb (590,000 kg) of illegal drugs and $27.9 million of drug money in 2003.

Bear Necessities

In 2004, a paralyzed Colorado man lay in bed unable to do anything while a 500-lb (227-kg) bear spent two hours ransacking his kitchen for snacks. Known in the area as "Fat Albert," the black bear helped himself to 4 lb (2 kg) of chocolate. Wildlife agents later found Albert sleeping off his sugar high in the man's dining room.

Ratty and Mole

Moles were causing a real problem in Lincolnshire, England, but when a man decided to hunt for them using his car headlights he wished he hadn't bothered. He crashed the car into his house, the fuel tank exploded, and his home burned to the ground.

Heavy Vetting

Americans spend more than six billion dollars per year on vets' fees.

Shrine to Swine

Outside a bungalow in Houston, Texas, are signs such as "No Porking," and "Pignic Area." A "pigup" truck stands in the driveway and the mailbox is shaped like a pig. The house is Pigdom—owner Victoria Herberta's own hog heaven. Victoria has had a lifelong fascination with pigs, particularly the famous Priscilla, which she taught to swim and sometimes shared a bed with. In 1984, Priscilla rescued a boy from drowning, leading to the creation of a "Priscilla the Pig Day" in Houston in the animal's honor. Although no longer allowed to keep pigs in the city, Victoria's devotion to them endures. "Pigs are intelligent, loving, and sensitive," she says. "I adore them."

Big Shot

A Michigan man shot at an opossum in his kitchen, but hit a gas line, causing an explosion that caused $45,000 worth of damage.

He'll Have You in Stitches

Baggio, a nine-year-old cockatiel, has stunned his tailor owner, Jack Territo, by learning to sew! The British bird learned his craft by mimicking his owner.

Bad Feather Day

Whipper the Budgie suffers from the bird version of a bad hair day, every day of his life. Born with a rare genetic mutation called "Feather Duster," Whipper was rejected by his parents and so was hand-reared by owner Julie Hayward.

Not only was he shunned by his own parents—Charles and Camilla—but also by other birds who live in the same New Zealand aviary. The story has a happy ending though, because Whipper now attracts an endless stream of visitors to his new home.

There have been only three cases of the "feather duster" syndrome recorded in the last 60 years.

Pet Dating

An internet dating agency in the U.K. offers to find companions for dogs—and possibly for their owners as well.

Costume Drama

Dog-owners in Nunoa, Chile, have started a trend of dressing their pets in fancy costumes when taking them for a walk. Dogs about town have been seen dressed as Batman and Robin, Easter bunnies, Cinderella, and Snow White. For more formal occasions, they have even been known to wear tuxedos or wedding dresses!

Steeple Chase

The Dog Chapel, East St. Johnsbury, Vermont, looks like an ordinary white clapboard church—except for the winged dog on the steeple, the stained-glass windows featuring canine characters, and the photographs commemorating dead pets on the walls.

Building up his Mussels

A Purdue University professor has discovered how mussels stick themselves to surfaces: They attach tiny filaments to objects that act like glue. He believes that this mussel "glue" could be used commercially in the future, perhaps in sealing wounds or in nerve reconstruction.

Frog March

Frog Fantasies is an unusual museum in Eureka Springs, Arkansas. It features nothing but frogs made from porcelain, wood, majolica, jade, coconut, cedar roots, and just about anything else you can think of.

Bundle of Fluff

Crystal is the biggest rabbit in the world, according to her owner Sue Dooley. The bumper British bunny weighs in at a whopping 27 lb (12 kg).

Coffin-bearer

In a record-breaking stunt, John Lamedica from Delaware U.S.A. lay down in a Plexiglas coffin… with more than 20,000 giant Madagascan hissing cockroaches to keep him company.

Cat Suits

A Japanese website offers tailor-made cat costumes to dress up your pet. Your cat could be a chick, a frog, a horse or, strangely, Anne of Green Gables.

Croc Climbing

A 13-ft (4-m) crocodile attempted to drag a man from his tent in Queensland, Australia, but was prevented from doing so by a daring 60-year-old woman who jumped on its back. Eventually, someone shot the crocodile. The man and woman both had to be treated for broken bones.

I Smell a Rat

Scientists at the University of Florida have identified neural signals that are transmitted by rats when they locate a scent. This means that eventually the rodents could be used to help in rescue attempts.

Groom Service

Luxury pet hotels offer condos and penthouse suites for dogs and cats, complete with ceiling fans and televisions. At PETSuites Pet Resort, pampered pets can also receive grooming and play sessions for an extra charge.

The Lamb and the Unicorn

John Turner of Haddon-on-the-Wall, England, discovered two bizarre looking lambs (below). One had two-heads and the other a horn!

Ripley's® —∞
TWO-HEADED LAMB
EXHIBIT NO: 19546
BORN WITH TWO
HEADS ON A FARM
IN ENGLAND

Ripley's® —∞
UNICORN LAMB
EXHIBIT NO: 19421
HAD A HORN STICKING OUT
OF ITS HEAD, WHICH MADE IT
LOOK LIKE A UNICORN

It Sticks out a Mile

Phoebe, a Malaysian giant stick insect, is the world's longest bug, measuring a massive 18 in (45 cm).

Make Yourself at Home

Bailey D. Buffalo spends more time in his owner's kitchen than in his shed!

Jim and Linda Sautner of Alberta, Canada, raised the buffalo from infancy, hence its tame nature. Bailey weighs 1,650 lb (748 kg), but visits the Sautner house every day. He enjoys privileges not usually experienced by buffalo—he's allowed into his owner's kitchen, although he rarely dines with them.

I Could Eat With a Horse

Ten-year-old Carissa Boulden watches her pet horse, Princess, eat a plate of spaghetti at the family's dining table in Sydney, Australia. Princess is even allowed to drink beer on Sundays!

The Lion in Winter

In 2003, Leon the "house lion" kept Radka Sarkanyova and her teddy bear company in the Czech Republic.

Do You Take This Dog...

After a "love at first sight" meeting while they were being walked by their owners, Saul, a Labrador guide dog, married Foxy, a Border Collie in August 2004 at a ceremony organized by Hollywood Hounds. The groom's best man looked on in awe as the bride made her entrance—traditionally late of course—accompanied by bridesmaids Misty, Cara, and Rena. The happy couple's marriage was then blessed by a vicar.

Drive Time

While his owner watched Canada win the 2004 World Hockey Cup, a dog managed to put a truck into gear and coast down a hill in Whitehorse, Yukon Territory. A man out for a walk alerted police after seeing the vehicle pass with a black Labrador Retriever at the wheel.

Rooster Boosters

Organizers of the 2001 New Mexico State Fair Rooster-crowing Contest blamed a quiet event on the heat. Spectators and owners flapped and clucked like chickens in a bid to stimulate activity, but the standard was so low that the winning rooster had to crow only twice.

Bubble Trouble

Connie Beck woke one morning in 2000 to hear strange noises in her home in Howard, Pennsylvania. Upon investigation, she found a deer taking a bubble bath in the bath tub! The deer had not only gained entry to the house, it had also managed to turn on the bathroom tap and knock over the bottle of bubble bath.

Hopping Mad

U.S. judge Randy Anglen was reported to be seeking compensation in 2004 after finding a dead mouse in a bottle of beer at his home in Hollister, Missouri. He had drunk the beer by the time he saw the rodent.

Slip into a Nice Bath

German angler Paul Richter doesn't have a rubber duck in his bath—he has been sharing the tub with a giant eel for the past 35 years. When he first caught the slippery creature, his children refused to allow him to cook and eat it. Although his children have now left home, Paul and his wife have become so fond of "Eelfie" that the intended supper has become a family pet that often joins them in the bath.

Can You Dig It?

After being hit by a mail delivery truck, Sweetie the dog showed no signs of life. Distraught owner Glenda Stevens dug a grave and buried her pet in the garden of her home in Park Hills, Missouri. However, hours later she was amazed to see Sweetie's hind legs sticking out of the ground. The dog, which had suffered a broken leg and jaw, was digging itself out of its own grave!

Faith Healer

Faith, a Labrador/Chow cross, was born without her two front legs and seemed destined to be destroyed. She was saved by Oklahoma City civil servant Jude Stringfellow, and has never looked back. Not only has she mastered the art of walking on two legs like a human being, but she has also become a celebrity—with her own agent, lawyer, and even a part in a Harry Potter movie.

Zebras Crossing

The second Baron Rothschild had a collection of exotic animals at his home in Buckinghamshire, England, in the late 19th century. It included kangaroos, a dingo, giant tortoises, and a team of four zebras that pulled his carriage.

A Meaty Treat

A Moscow company makes meat-based birthday cakes for dogs. They cost about $60.

A Day They'll Never Forget

Two pairs of elephants were married in a lavish Valentine's Day ceremony in Ayuthaya, Thailand, in 2001. The elephants wore gowns embroidered with red hearts and even had their trunks brightly painted for the special occasion.

Make it Snappy

When Erroberto Piza Rios fancies a game of soccer, he chooses opponents who have a tendency to snap—his pet crocodiles. Erroberto delights tourists on the beach at Iztapa, Mexico, by kicking a ball around with the reptiles, all of which are named after former soccer stars. His favorite trick is to place the ball on one of their heads so that they can lift their powerful jaws and let it roll down their back. He claims never to have been attacked and, in another demonstration, intrigues onlookers by allowing a small crocodile to bite his face gently.

On His Last Legs

Boontawee Siengwong, of Bangkok, Thailand, spent 28 days and nights eating and sleeping with 1,000 centipedes in a glass room measuring just 129 sq ft (12 sq m).

The Odd Couple

An orphaned baby hippopotamus has adopted a 100-year-old tortoise as its surrogate mother. The hippo, Owen, which weighs about 650 lb (300 kg), follows the giant tortoise everywhere, and becomes angry and protective whenever the tortoise is approached. They live together at an animal facility in Mombasa, Kenya, Africa.

On All Fours

This cockerel was born in Tirana, Albania, with four legs—two too many.

What Are you Like?

Can't Stomach It!

Strongman Jess Caigoy is known as the Human Vacuum Cleaner!

Jess feasts on a variety of unpalatable items, including worms and grubs, washes them all down, and then regurgitates them using a long

Jess inserts the tube after he's feasted enough!

Jess starts by helping himself to a range of unusual appetizers!

He washes them down.

He throws his head back to make sure they go down.

Jess prepares for the regurgitation by passing the tube down his throat.

plastic surgery before she met him. He promptly divorced her and sued her for fraud.

Sweaty Socks

A pair of Canadian rock star Bryan Adams's sweaty socks sold for over $1,000 on eBay. Adams accidentally left the black Armani socks behind when changing for a concert, but gave permission for the unwashed footwear to be sold.

Smile Please

Toothless police officers in the Philippines were issued free dentures in 2005 as part of a drive to encourage them to smile more!

You've Gotta Hand it to Him

Vietnam veteran Bob Wieland is a regular competitor in U.S. marathons—even though he has no legs. Bob covers the 26 mi (42 km) on his hands, using a special pair of "hand shoes," made of gel and attached by leather straps.

What a Picture

Paul Morris paid more than £10,000 ($19,000) to have the whole of his upper body and head tattooed.

The Ugly Truth

Jian Feng of Hegang, northern China, was suspicious when his wife gave birth to an ugly baby. Then his wife confessed—not to adultery, but to having undergone major

Brave Bob propelled only by his hands, crossed America in 3 years, 8 months and 6 days in the 1980s. He admits it's hard going, and says: "One mile on your hands is like 25 miles on your legs."

Check Mate

Matt Gone is a walking, talking checkerboard. Since 1990, the New Orleans dishwasher has had 300 hours of tattoo sessions, costing $44,000, to cover his body in black-and-white squares. The design, conceived to hide unsightly birthmarks, now covers 94 per cent of Matt's body. Only his face, hands, and the soles of his feet are untouched. For variety, one leg is covered with water designs, the other with images of fire. "I see it as an art form," he says. "I'm wearing my portfolio."

Bottle Neck

Circus of Horrors performer Satanica can fit into a bottle as part of her act with Docktor Haze.

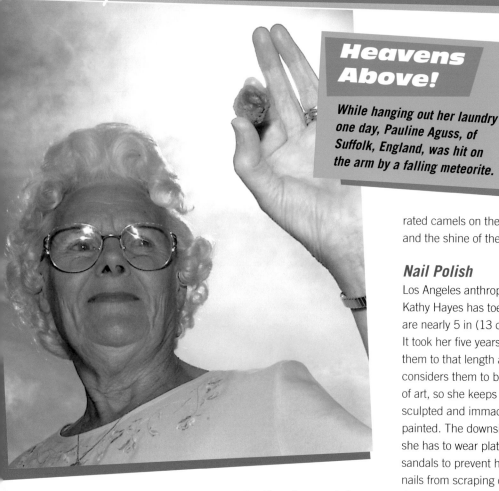

rated camels on their humps and the shine of their hair.

Nail Polish

Los Angeles anthropologist Kathy Hayes has toenails that are nearly 5 in (13 cm) long. It took her five years to grow them to that length and she considers them to be a work of art, so she keeps them sculpted and immaculately painted. The downside is that she has to wear platform sandals to prevent her nails from scraping on the ground.

The Human Slate

Rosa Barthelme was known as "the Human Slate" because she could etch words into the skin on her back that would stay there for several minutes.

Fastest Finger

Hairdresser Valentino LoSauro, of Fort Myers, Florida, is a real-life Scissorhands. He has invented a device called "Clawz," which consists of ten mini razors attached to his fingertips. Since the contraption allows each finger to cut independently, he can do the work of ten hairdressers and saves considerable time.

They've Got the Hump

The first international camel beauty pageant was held in Mongolia in 2003. Herders

The Milky Way

Ilker Yilmaz, from Turkey, can squirt milk from his eye as far as 110 in (280 cm).

Smile!

Fancy flashing those pearly whites to reveal an artistic touch?

Tooth art could have you smiling to show off your pretty premolars after art dentist Ron Grant has had a chance to work his artistic magic in your mouth.

Eye Eye

If adorning your teeth isn't your thing, perhaps eye art might be. Eyeball jewelry will have people gazing into your eyes!

Illustrations can include patriotic flying flags, famous icons, and celebrities, or they can pay homage to your favorite musicians and bands.

Licked Into Shape

German schoolgirl Annika Irmler reckons that, at 3 in (7 cm), her tongue is the longest in the world. She can even lick ice-cream from the bottom of a cone!

Korean Trim

The government of North Korea has waged war on men with long hair, calling them unhygienic and "blind followers of bourgeois lifestyle." Under the new regulations, men must wear their hair no longer than 2 in (5 cm), the only concession being to old men who can grow it up to 3 in (7 cm) to cover baldness. Violators risk being named and shamed on national TV.

Glowing Praise

San Francisco tattoo artist Greg Kulz uses homemade tattoo ink to give people tattoos that glow in the dark.

Double Booking

Canadian police officer Chris Legere booked identical twins for speeding on the same day—in the same car! One morning in January 2005 he pulled over an 18-year-old woman from Akwesasne for driving at 96 mph (154 km/h).

Then in the afternoon he stopped the same car doing 92 mph (148 km/h) in the opposite direction. He first thought it was the same driver but identity checks showed that it was her twin sister.

Tall Order

A club for Indian men over 6 ft (1.8 m) tall announced in 2003 that it was opening its doors to women because members have difficulty finding brides. In a country where the average male height is 5 ft 7 in (1.7 m), the club in the southern state of Kerala has attracted some 300 members. One says: "Tall people are just a laughing-stock in India. In cinema halls, we have to insist on back rows. On buses, we can't even stand properly."

Jaw and Order

In a landmark operation, surgeons in Golden, Colorado, have fitted teenager Mandy Kemp with a prosthetic jaw. Mandy, who suffers from Goldenhar Syndrome, a rare genetic disorder that leaves the face looking lopsided, was fitted with a cobalt-chromium implant after 3-D imaging was used to create an exact replica of her skull and facial bones.

Two Heads are Better Than One

A two-headed goat was born in Bauta, Cuba, in May 2004. Its owner, Juan Bolanos, reported that the goat could breathe and feed with both heads, and opened and closed all four of its eyes at the same time!

On Your Marx

In May 2003, 800 students and faculty members at East Lansing High School, Michigan, gathered for the biggest-ever Groucho Marx tribute. They all wore sets of Groucho glasses, fuzzy eyebrows, and mustaches.

Fan Male

Chris Gennaro, 31, gave up a career as a doctor—so he could dress like Madonna! His obsession began when he saw the dress for 1984's "Like a Virgin." Since giving up medicine, he has worked as a waiter, and spent his time and $100,000 going to see Madonna and recreating 100 of her outfits on the sewing-machine in his Brooklyn apartment.

You're Busted

In 2004, sculptor Rich Varano molded busts of presidential candidates John Kerry and George Bush out of hummus. Varano also sculpted a flat version of Bush (left)—out of the same unusual material!

Piped Music

In the 1930s, Charles Gregory, half of popular vaudeville act Gregory and Damon, played popular dance tunes on a Eureka vacuum cleaner—no other make would do.

EUREKA DE LUXE

Going to Pieces

The Enigma, for many years a member of The Jim Rose Circus, has his entire body covered with a blue jigsaw-puzzle tattoo. To complete his highly individual look, the American performer has also had horns implanted in the skin surrounding his skull!

Ducking Out

A Sao Paulo prisoner who tried to escape from jail dressed as a woman was caught because he couldn't walk in high heels. Guards at Taquaritinga Prison said Moacir Pacagnan looked like a pretty woman but waddled like a duck.

Seeing is Believing

German businessman Ralph Anderl has invented a unique pair of spectacles—"Sushi Specs." The unusual glasses have detachable arms that can be used as chopsticks!

True or False?

While fishing at Appling, Georgia, 70-year-old Verdell James sneezed violently and watched in horror as his $300 false teeth dropped into Thurmond Lake. Police rescue divers returned them two days later.

Hair Apparent

Hans Naumann holds the trophy for the longest mustache in the European Contest of Beards and Mustaches. At 5 ft (1.5 m) long, his 'tache was a real winner. The use of artificial styling aids, including mustache wax, hairspray, hair gel, and styling cream, is strictly forbidden.

Sidewalk Show

German artists Edgar Müller and Manfred Stader have drawn crowds worldwide with their impressive and unique three-dimensional street art.

Their works of art include raging waterfalls, low-flying helicopters, and shark attacks.

Using chalk and paint the two artists create eye-deceiving pavement drawings that are unbelievably lifelike. One piece of work, measuring 919 sq ft (208 sq m), saw them turning a byway called River Street into a river complete with waterfall on which a raft appears to be about to plummet into a raging torrent.

> It took Muller and Stader three days to complete this work using paint.

Watch where you walk—one wrong step and you might find yourself falling from the sky into Berlin's secret city. The piece titled "Stunt City" took four days to finish and was a massive 49 x 82 ft (15 x 25 m) in size.

The Boy Who Never Grew Up

Randy Constan lives in his own Never Never Land. The 50-year-old from Britain is so obsessed with Peter Pan that for the past 30 years he has worn green tights. His fixation, which includes climbing trees and leaping from them in a bid to emulate his hero, has seen him lose both his wife and his job. "Being Peter Pan is part of my life," he says. "When I was eight I told my dad I wanted to be a fairy."

Stretch Your Legs

Teenager Emma Richards, from Cornwall, England, underwent a six-hour operation in 2000 to have her legs stretched. She wanted to increase her height from 4 ft 9 in (1.45 m) to 5 ft 2 in (1.6 m) so that she could achieve her ambition of becoming a flight attendant.

Window Pain

Tattoo artist Miranda Griffiths, of Washington, D.C., sports self-designed tattoos of stained-glass windows on her lower legs.

Rogue Mail

Here's proof that Bill Clinton didn't think much of online correspondence during his presidency—he sent only two e-mails during his entire term in office. In comparison, his staff sent just under 40 million. One of his e-mails was to test the system, while the second was sent to astronaut John Glenn to congratulate him on his return to space. Both e-mails are now archived in the Bill Clinton Presidential Library.

He Spoke Too Soon

At the Phuket Vegetarian Festival in Thailand, pierced participants parade through the streets to show their devotion to their religion. Their piercings are adorned with objects including swords, skewers, branches —and even a bicycle.

The Mane Attraction

Known as "Lionel the Lion-faced Boy," Stephen Bilgraski was born in Russia in the mid-19th century, and later performed in the U.S.A. with Barnum and Bailey's circus. He claimed his condition was caused by his mother seeing his father killed by a lion while she was pregnant, but we now know it was a result of a rare genetic disorder called hypertrichosis, or werewolf syndrome.

Gnarly Nails

Murari Aditya of Calcutta, India, let the fingernails on his left hand grow to a combined length of 54¼ inches (138 cm). He also made small lizards and insects from his nail clippings!

Snakes Alive
The latest trend among New York society women is to carry live snakes as an accessory! The snakes are usually carried in handbags and are chosen for their color—green garters and bright-banded corn snakes have proven particularly popular.

Ear, Ear
Many a man is proud of his long hair, but B.D. Tyagi of Bhopal, India, rejoices at the length of his ear hair. Wild and wiry, it sprouts an amazing 4 in (10 cm) from his outer ear.

Center Forward
Pregnant women who like to show off their bellies have a firm ally in American artist Laurie Steinfeld. He makes sure their expanded bellies really do stand out by painting them to resemble soccer balls or basketballs.

Tough Talk
Who says Klingons can't spread peace? On *Star Trek* they are short-tempered thugs who live for battle, but San Diego Trekkies known as "the Imperial Klingon Vessel Stranglehold" visit schools dressed in full Klingon garb to talk about how to solve squabbles. They believe kids can learn from the culture's strict code of honor.

All Fingers and Toes

In the 1920s, all the villagers in Cervera de Buitrago, Spain, had extra digits.

Green Nose

When a four-year-old Romanian boy went for a routine check-up in 2003, doctors found a plant growing from his nose! The boy, from a mountain village, hadn't complained about the bean, which even had little leaves.

Guilty Secret

A man from Long Beach, Mississippi, was convicted of armed robbery in 2003 after being identified by tattoos including a gun on his neck and the words "not guilty."

Playing Hard Ball

Alex Ednie had an amazing super-strong golf swing— he could shoot balls right through a phone book!

Revolving Head

Known as "The Human Owl," Martin Laurello could turn his whole head 180° to look backward, leaving his body facing forward. Astonishingly, Laurello could still walk forward, without falling over, while revolving his head in the opposite direction!

Let Your Hair Down

After 38 years without a haircut, Tran Van Hay from Vietnam has hair more than 20⅓ ft (6.2 m) in length!

A School for Santas

The "Ministry of Fun Santa School" in London, England, hosted a training day to enable professional Santa Claus performers to fine-tune their festive duties!

Pins and Needles

Brent Moffatt has turned himself into a human pincushion. In December 2003, Moffatt, who lives in Moose Jaw, Saskatchewan, inserted 900 surgical needles into his leg simultaneously. This amazing total easily surpassed his previous record of 702 body piercings. Although Brent admits that there were a few trickles of blood, he insisted that he felt no pain. "It just felt like a whole bunch of little ants crawling over me," he declared stoically.

Spelling Test

Lee Williams of Roseville, Michigan, sued a tattoo parlor for $25,000 in 1999 for misspelling a tattoo on his right forearm. The word "villain" came out as "villian" because neither Williams nor the tattooist knew how to spell it at the time.

Making a Point

A Chinese man has had plastic surgery to give him pointed ears like *Star Trek*'s Mr. Spock. The young man astonished surgeons in Nanjing when he told them he wanted alien-like ears because he was bored with their current shape. Despite their misgivings, the surgeons decided to go ahead with the operation.

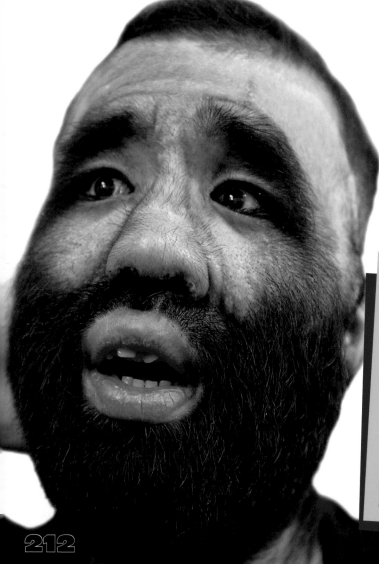

Rolling in the Aisles

It wasn't a church aisle that checkout-operator Jill Piggot went up when she married fellow supermarket worker Pete Freeman in 2004—it was a supermarket aisle!

Hold Your Horses

Cosmetic tattoo artist Teri Reid is used to a wide variety of customers, but she never expected to tattoo a horse! As a break from her usual clientele, Teri, from Twin Falls, Idaho, treats American paint horses whose pale coats leave little natural pigmentation around the eyes. When they are exposed to sunlight, the glare can cause serious eye problems. So Teri puts the horses under anesthetic and applies permanent black eyeliner. "It's like giving a horse a pair of sunglasses," she says.

Swine Fever

Norwegian pig farmer Arne Braut started wearing a pig mask and grunting at his swine in the hope of forging a closer relationship with them. He claims that they are much calmer when they think he is another pig.

Hair and Now

Officially China's hairiest man, Yu Zhenhuan's body is 96 per cent covered in hair. Twenty-six-year-old Yu recently underwent surgery to remove some hair from his ear, which had caused hearing loss. Doctors believe he has an average of 41 hairs per 0.15 sq in (1 sq cm).

A Bit of Fluff

Priscella, known as "Monkey Girl," had a completely hairy body and a full beard. She was married to circus performer "Emmett, the alligator-skinned man," and together they performed with the Calvacade of Amusements at Coney Island in the 1920s.

Bearded Lady

Set up by computer programmer Jerry Jackson, the Internet's National Beard Registry features more than 250 hairy Americans. Jerry wanted the site to show that it's OK to grow facial hair, no matter what the boss thinks. In 2004, the first whiskered woman joined—a 26-year-old from Philadelphia with a short brown goatee that she had been growing for just over a year.

Picture This

Julia Gnuse of Los Angeles, California, began tattooing her body in 1991 in order to conceal the effects of a rare skin condition. She is now tattooed from the top of her head right down to her ankles—including her face and fingers—mainly with figures from television and the movies.

Human Kebabs

Worshipers in Malaysia celebrate at the annual Thaipusam festival near Kuala Lumpur by hooking and sticking skewers through their own skin to the accompaniment of deafening music that apparently helps to ease the pain.

My Left Feet

Japanese police arrested 45-year-old Ichiro Irie in October 2003—after 440 women's left shoes were found in his home. "I have always been interested in women's feet," he explained to police. They remained baffled, however, about his preference for left feet.

Fat Cat

In August 2004, Dr. Robert Ersek, who is better known as "the biggest fat-sucker in Austin, Texas," performed liposuction in front of television cameras—on himself! The American plastic surgeon performed this feat as part of his program of promoting the potential use of stem cells, which can be harvested in such operations. As the 66-year-old sucked fat cells out of his belly, he said: "We're doing our part to keep Austin weird."

Hair Style

A Romanian woman makes clothes from her own hair! Ioana Cioanca has been saving every hair that falls out for nearly 50 years, ever since her grandmother told her it was a sin to throw it away. She now has an entire wardrobe of hair fashion, including a raincoat, waistcoat, blouse, skirt, hat, and a matching handbag.

He's for the Chop

On October 16, 2004, the unbelievable strength of karate instructor Mike Reeves was proved yet again when, in front of the Ripley Museum in Orlando, he broke 1,534 1-in (2.5-cm) thick boards in just 10 minutes 12 seconds.

Chainsaw Art

Carroll Sanders, of Hawesville, Kentucky, risks life and limb to carve letters on to his toenails—using a full-size chainsaw.

Hero Worship

Belgian Emmanuel de Reyghere has had nine operations to make him look like Michael Jackson. "Some people spend their money on golf," he says. "I just spend all my money on making my face look like Michael's." His girlfriend left him five years ago.

Blooming Marvelous

U.S. hair-stylist Kevin Carter from Southfield, Michigan, is renowned for his ability to turn hair into floral arrangements. At Hair Wars 2000, in Detroit, he spent nearly three hours turning a model into a vase for a 2-ft (0.6-m) high sansevieria plant made of hair. First he stitched the plant to a fabric base that was stitched to the model's hair, then he combed and sprayed her hair so that it blended into the plant.

The Boy with Two Brains

An Afghan woman gave birth to a two-headed boy in Iran in August 2004. Najmeh Wahedian's son was born of a cesarean section with an apparently normal body, but with two separate heads on his shoulders. Medical tests showed that the baby had two functioning brains, each controlling one side of the body, two hearts, and two spinal cords. Sometimes one head would cry while the other one slept.

Bra Constrictor

Customs officers in Stockholm, Sweden, arrested a woman who tried to smuggle 75 live snakes in her bra. The officers were suspicious as the woman kept scratching her chest.

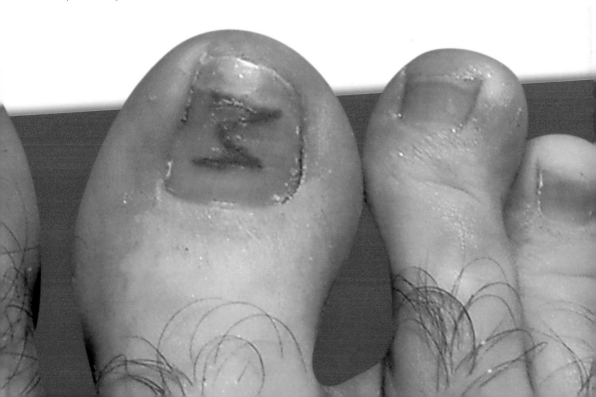

Record Achievement

Before he died at the age of 18, Bryan Naranjo stood just under 28 in (71 cm) tall. Bryan, from Colombia, was one of the shortest men in South America.

Goodness Nose

A campaign launched in Los Angeles in 2002 included a "Show off your Nose" contest, in which officials measured and recorded details of noses of all shapes and sizes.

Lady Gray

Rosemary Jacobs, from Atlanta, Georgia, has a rare skin condition called argyria, which has turned her skin gray. She thinks it's a result of nose drops she took as a child, which contained silver.

Turtle Mutates

Michele Ivey, of Ferndale, Michigan, sees herself as the fifth Ninja Turtle. At the age of 11, she fell in love with Michelangelo, the green-masked party dude of the Teenage Mutant Ninja Turtles, and she's spent the past 15 years chasing her obsession. In that time she has spent $5,000 on karate lessons, and has even bought a replica head of Michelangelo to wear. She says the turtles give her inner strength.

New Moon

In 1934 Clyde Van Patten, an evangelist from Michigan, attracted massive crowds to hear his sermons. The reason for the wide attraction was because he promised to perform songs—using just his nose.

It's a Cover-up

Toronto Blue Jays pitcher Justin Miller was told to cover up the multicolored tattoos on his left arm after umpires ruled that they were proving a distraction to hitters.

219

What a Catch

Al Green of the Bronx, New York, caught 26 foul balls at Brooklyn Dodgers games in 1946. Over the next four years, he caught 211 balls at Dodgers, Giants, and Yankees games. Al worked nights and so could go to games in both the afternoon and evening.

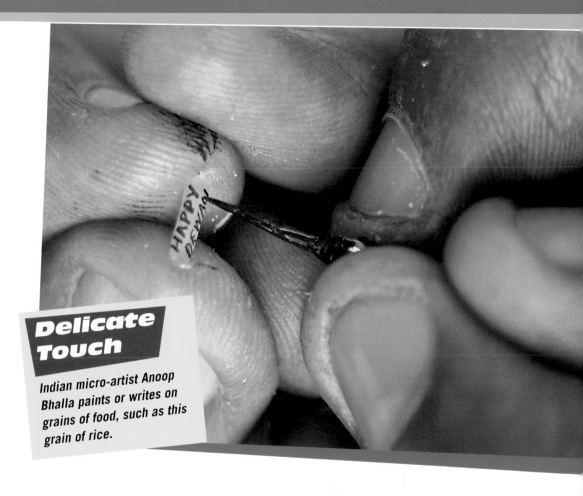

Delicate Touch

Indian micro-artist Anoop Bhalla paints or writes on grains of food, such as this grain of rice.

I.D. Tag

T.D. Rockwell, from San Francisco had his own name and address—as well as that of his bank—tattooed on his leg in 27 languages, including Morse Code and semaphore.

Double Trouble

A ten-year-old boy got the shock of his life in 2003 when he stumbled across a two-headed snake. Hunter York, of Centertown, Kentucky, took the non-venomous king snake home to look after it, but his family didn't know which head to feed.

A Full Moon

Railroad passengers going through Laguna Niguel, California, on the second Saturday in July always see a full moon. In a bizarre annual ceremony, hundreds of drinkers from the nearby Mugs Away Saloon drop their trousers and bare their bottoms at the 25 trains that pass through that day. It began in 1979, when K.T. Smith offered to buy a drink for anyone willing to moon the next train. Moon Amtrak is now so popular that for that Saturday trains are booked solid for months in advance.

Painted Lady

Body-painters from all over the world flocked to Austria in 2004 to see the many wonders on display.

Body artists were able to capture the mythical theme using various techniques.

The World Body-painting Festival ran a myths, fairy tales, and water theme, which resulted in some spectacular sights and a magical atmosphere.

Half human, half alien, using body paint, costumes, and accessories only.

223

On Ice

In 1989, Trygve Bauge, a resident of Nederland, Colorado, had the body of his dead grandfather shipped from Norway and packed in ice in a shed so that he could resurrect him in the future. Tygve was subsequently deported, but Grandpa Bredo was allowed to remain in Nederland and, although his body has not been seen for some years, his presence is celebrated by the town each March on Frozen Dead Guy Day. Events include a coffin race, a snow-sculpting contest, Grandpa lookalike competitions, and guided tours to the shed.

A Twist in the Nail

India's Romesh Sharma shows off his fingernails, which are a staggering 33 ft (10 m) long. Romesh's talons set a new world record in New Delhi in 2003 easily breaking the previous record of 20 ft 2 in (6.15 m).

Choc Full

On February 14, 1997, chocoholics Melanie Lugo and Kevin Kuhlman tied the knot while sitting in a bathtub that had been filled with cooled liquid chocolate. The couple, who were married by Rev. Stern, arranged for a restaurant in New York to prepare the chocolate in advance.

Francisco's Solid Waste Transfer and Recycling Center, which is otherwise known as the city dump. Every artist brings their own specialty to the position. Carpenter says he is creating art from discarded bulk items, and cites the weaving he made from 40 orange extension cords.

Doppelgangers

Vivian Weiss and Joseph Pepper were both residents in the same city in Nebraska. However, they had more in common than they realized: after often being mistaken for each other, they met at a party, where they discovered that they not only shared a birthday, but also an anniversary and stomach complaints, and they had children of similar ages, and liked and disliked the same kinds of foods!

Modern Art is Trash

Sculptor Rick Carpenter is the 43rd artist to hold the title "Artist in Residence" at San

Wind Bags

Some people will buy anything from eBay. Recent bidders agreed to pay $10 for wind "captured" from Hurricane Frances and stored in Tupperware containers.

Bald is Beautiful

Ever since he started losing his hair at 15, John Capps has

believed that bald is beautiful. He is clearly not alone, as his society, Bald Headed Men of America, boasts more than 35,000 members. Each year, they meet in Morehead City, North Carolina, for the Bald is Beautiful Convention. As Capps says: "Morehead means less hair."

Top That

The longest beard chain in the world was created by two men called Chervalier and Schaffer in Stuttgart, Germany. Twenty bearded participants tied their beards together, creating the longest beard chain ever recorded—a massive 78⅔ ft (24 m)!

Knife and Fork

Seth Griffin speaks with a forked tongue—literally. A friend used a scalpel to split the tongue of the 29-year-old body-piercer from Bay City, Michigan. He also has three Teflon domes implanted in his chest, and more than 30 piercings on his body, including the bridge of his nose, and his eyebrows, nipples, lips, septum, and ears. "It's not a fashion statement," says Seth with a slight lisp. "It's about feeling good about myself. I feel I am different from other people, so I set myself apart by changing the way I look."

Shake a Leg

David Spinler, a farmer from Freeborn County, Minnesota, had been told by the vet to expect his cow to have twin calves in 2004. Instead, there was just one calf, but it had an extra two legs protruding from its back. Sadly, the six-legged animal died during birth, but David was so intrigued by it that he decided to have it preserved by a taxidermist.

Rope Warrior

Jumping rope has never been quite so spectacular!

David Fisher, "The Rope Warrior," makes amazing stunts look simple—like "tush-ups," jumping rope while bouncing on his behind, and dribbling a ball at the same time. Not only can he perform a great range of stunts, but he can also speed-jump at more than 100 mph (160 km/h)! David has made more than 75 television appearances. He performed at President George W. Bush's first inauguration, and attends school assemblies every week to stress the importance of teamwork and physical fitness.

"My Ropenastics program is inexpensive, portable, infinite in its creative possibilities, and is one of the best cardiovascular workouts one can get," claims David.

The Story of Omi

Omi the Tattooed Man was covered in tattoos from the top of his head to the soles of his feet. Sometimes billed as a Maori when he performed at Ripley's Odditorium in New York City in 1939, he was actually a British World War I recruit.

Art and Sole

You might think fishy footwear means soles and 'eels, but English designer Oliver Sweeney has created a men's shoe made from a stingray. The skin of the flat fish forms the uppers, and the shoes have a traditional leather sole. The fishy shoes sell for £750 ($1,500) a pair.

Super Surgeon

Lebanese doctor Ira Kahn had an inflamed appendix and was on his way to the hospital, but got stuck in a traffic jam. When he realized that it would take him too long to get to the hospital, he made a risky decision—he performed emergency surgery on himself to remove his appendix.

Something for Nothing

Ted Mattison went without food, shelter, water, sunblock—and clothes—during a recent week-long festival in the Nevada desert. Why? To gauge the kindness of others. Fortunately for Matthison, he found that people are basically generous: within hours he was given food and water, and within days he acquired a complete campsite.

Kiss and Tell

Catherine Wagner, 69, of Ohio, has finally become a member of her high school honor society. She was barred from membership 51 years ago because she was caught in the school hall kissing her boyfriend—to whom she has now been married for more than 40 years. It was only last year, at her 50th high school reunion, that the current principal learned of her snub and saw to it that she was inducted.

Two of a Kind

Twins Reba and Lori Schappell, 44, are incredibly close yet have never seen each other's faces without a mirror. Joined at the head, they face in opposite directions. The twins from Reading, Pennsylvania, who also have to use a mirror to watch TV together, share 30 per cent of their brain tissue, as well as one non-functional eye. Nevertheless they have managed to lead normal lives. Reba is a country singer while Lori worked part-time in a hospital laundry until she quit to support her sister's music career.

Back to Front

Pierre Beauchemin, of France, was more than your average contortionist—not only was he able to scratch his ears with his feet, he could also turn his legs around so that he appeared to walk backward while moving forward!

All-

Consuming

Ummm... Nice!?!

Matthew Biancaniello proved that he can eat anything during a 2002 Ripley's TV show.

Matthew takes a pause before consuming yet another sumptuous snack!

Matthew considers the many delicacies he intends to devour during his act.

Matthew's feat is not for the weak-stomached to watch! His eat-anything menu includes such treats as animal eyeballs, cow dung, a cow's and bull's muscles, leeches, maggots, and fish intestines.

Matthew gets stuck on to a chewy treat.

I believe that's an eyeball he's eating!

Grubs, maggots, and worms... delicious!

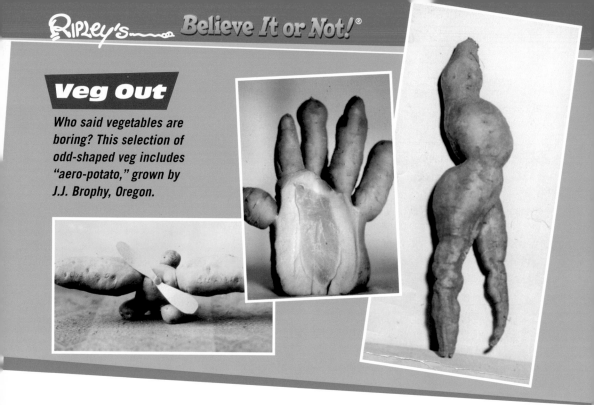

Veg Out

Who said vegetables are boring? This selection of odd-shaped veg includes "aero-potato," grown by J.J. Brophy, Oregon.

A Light Lunch

An Indian man has been eating pieces of glass and empty liquor bottles for the past 20 years. P. Arthanari Swamy found he could digest glass when he crushed some in his drink during a failed suicide attempt. Now his mother often serves him glass bulbs and bottles with his dinner. The only glass items he can't eat are soda bottles, which are too thick. When he wants a change, he eats lead bullets!

Make Yourself at Home

A burglar broke into a dozen Seattle homes in August 2004 to raid... the refrigerators. Ignoring the jewelry, in one home he ate six shrimp kebabs, 12 mini corndogs, half a pack of cooked meat, 12 balls of frozen cookie dough, handfuls of candies, a box of Creamsicles, two fruit drinks, and a glass of milk. In another break-in he thawed and fried frozen steaks and ate them while watching TV—until he was disturbed by the homeowners!

Don't Forget to Floss

Diane DeCair of Toledo, Ohio, likes to inhale strands of spaghetti up her nose. In fact, by carefully sniffing and coughing, she can simultaneously pull one end of the pasta from her nose and the other from her mouth, in a flossing motion. "It's kind of disgusting to watch," she admits.

The Spitting Image

The International Cherry Pit Spitting Championship at Eau Claire, Michigan, has turned into a real family affair. Rick Krause has won the title 12 times, and in 2004 his son Brian completed a hat-trick of wins with a spit of 88 ft 2 in (26.8 m), just 5 ft (1.5 m) short of his 2003 record. Rick actually married his wife Marlene at the contest. Naturally, she's an ace spitter too.

Forever Blowing Bubbles

Susan Montgomery Williams of Fresno, California, has been America's "Bubble Queen" since 1979. After discovering that the existing record for blowing bubblegum was a modest 17 in (43 cm) bubble, Susan told the Bubble Yum Company that she could blow a 20 in (50 cm) bubble with just three pieces of gum. They didn't believe her, until she arrived blowing a bubble the size of a basketball with one breath. She won an unlimited supply of bubblegum as long as she held the record. Over 25 years later, she still holds it with a blow of 23 in (58 cm).

Burns' Night Blast-off

In 2002, Canadian businessman Gordon Sinclair announced that, as part of the Robert Burns' Night celebrations, he had patented a Haggis Launcher in order to propel a 1 lb (454 g) haggis across Calgary's huge Bow River!

A Sting in the Tale

Dorset, England, is home to the World Stinging Nettle Eating Championships, in which competitors eat their way through the stinging, itching plant. Ouch!

Hold the Mayo!

Weighing 6,991 lb (3,171 kg), this giant sandwich was made by workers in Mexico City in 2004.

Lord of the Flies

A man named Farook has taken to eating a diet consisting solely of flies in protest at his council's garbage-collection service. The social worker says that rotting garbage left in the streets of Tirunelveli, western India, is attracting swarms of the insects.

Hen-pecked

Jan Csovary, from Prievidza, Slovakia, has eaten more than 11,000 chickens since being diagnosed as a diabetic in the early 1970s. He has chicken for breakfast, lunch, and tea, but has to cook it himself because his wife moaned that she was sick of the sight of chickens 20 years ago!

In the Soup

In Erie, Pennsylvania, Democrats at the Polish Falcons Club eat duck blood soup every election day!

Spuds They Like

Every year, the town of Clark, South Dakota, stages a Potato Day in celebration of its favorite vegetable. The festivities include a Best Decorated Potato contest, potato sculptures and mashed-potato wrestling,

in which the combatants fight each other in a ring full of mashed potato.

Big Mouth

In 1998, American Johnny Reitz managed to cram three standard-sized hamburgers (including buns) into his mouth simultaneously without swallowing.

Carrot and Stick

Julie Tori, from Southampton, England, has eaten between 4 lb (1.8 kg) and 5 lb (2.3 kg) of carrots every day for the past ten years. She did have one day off from munching her favorite vegetable—but was immediately seized by a panic attack.

Dynamic Duo

According to a recent survey by Mr. Clean and Magic Eraser, Americans simply can't resist spaghetti and meatballs. The dish took the title for "Favorite Food Duo," and macaroni and cheese, and milk and cereal were a close second and third.

Pie in the Sky

According to Domino's Pizza, the five biggest days for pizza delivery in the U.S.A. are Super Bowl Sunday,

Thanksgiving Eve, New Year's Day, New Year's Eve, and Halloween. Every week, Domino's drivers rack up 9 million mi (13.5 million km), which is further than 37 trips to the Moon and back.

Hard Graft

Paramedics in Stuart, Florida, worked up a sweat when trying to remove a 480-lb (218-kg) woman from her home. They knew the doorways would be tricky, but quickly discovered a much more pressing problem. The woman, who had not moved from her couch for several years, had to be carried out on it because the fabric had grafted on to her skin. Doctors surgically separated the woman from the couch, but she died in the hospital after breathing complications.

Bearing Fruit

Camilla Bowitz from Worcester, England, had a special fruit tree growing in her back garden—it bore both apples and plums!

Hair-brained Scheme

Gary Arnold has a unique method of charging customers who visit his restaurant in Lodi, California—he charges them according to the amount of hair on their head. The hairiest pay most, and bald people eat for free!

A Brush with Death

Surgeons in India removed a toothbrush from a man's stomach a week after he accidentally swallowed it. Anil Kumar apparently swallowed the toothbrush while brushing his teeth in front of the TV, but went to the hospital only when the pain became unbearable.

Impeccable Taste

Wilma Beth Shulke, of Mission, Texas, created her own Easter outfit made from sliced cross-sections of corn cobs, trimmed with orange peel.

Dip In

While 20 per cent of the U.S.A.'s population eat 48 per cent of the avocados consumed each year, Super Bowl Sunday is the biggest day of the year for avocado consumption. Industry executives estimate that more than 43 million lb (19.5 million kg) are eaten during the football game, most of it in the form of guacamole dip.

Dog Eat Dog

At age ten, "Krazy" Kevin Lipsitz from Staten Island, New York, could eat ten ears of corn in a sitting. Now a speed-eating champ, he once ate 2 lb (1 kg) of sour pickles in five minutes, and his wife, Lorain, also competes as "Loraineasaurus Rex." Kevin trains with his two dogs. "I cook up a family pack of 40 hot dogs and we race. But we don't eat out of the same bowl."

Sweet as Candy

Slater Barron's friends and neighbors collect lint for her, which she stores in boxes in her studio/garage. She then sorts the lint according to color before creating the art.

Ripley's

LINT ART
EXHIBIT NO: 13989
SUSHI AND CANDY MADE
BY SLATER BARRON ENTIRELY
OUT OF LINT

Dressing for Dinner

Fashion designer Alessandro Consiglio cooked up a storm on the runways of Rome, Italy, in 2002.

Using vacuum-packed meat (including salami, ham, and pastrami) instead of conventional fabrics, the exotic fashion designer created a feast for more than just the eyes, as models showed off the meaty masterpieces to applauding onlookers.

Bread Winner

As part of his *Pain Couture* exhibition in Paris, fashion designer Jean Paul Gaultier celebrated the artistry of French bakers by creating dresses, boots, bags, and even thongs, from dough.

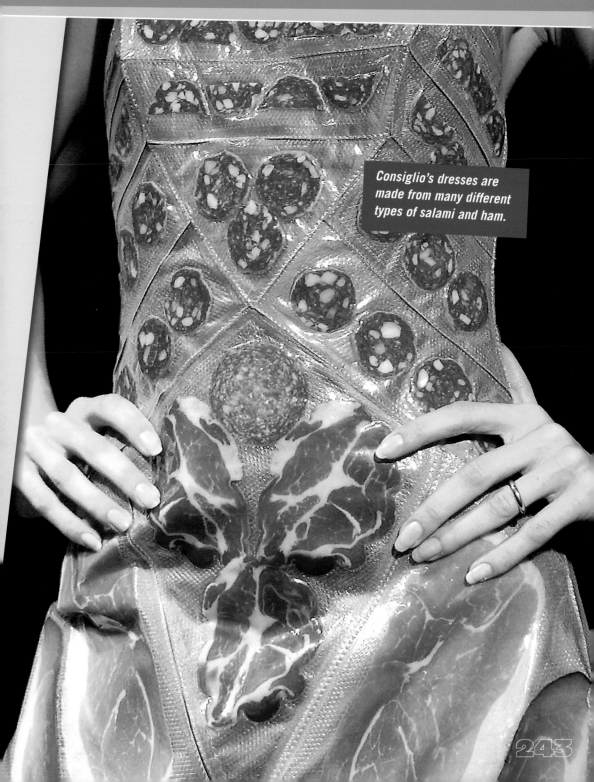

Consiglio's dresses are made from many different types of salami and ham.

A Man of Beans

Barry Kirk, aka Captain Beany, is bean mad! He loves baked beans so much that he has officially changed his name to Captain Beany.

He drives a baked-bean illustrated car, drinks baked-bean cocktails, paints himself orange, and dons a baked-bean costume!

He wears an orange jumpsuit and cape and even paints his bald head orange. When he needed a passport to match his new identity, he produced a completely orange photo of himself. Naturally, he eats baked beans every day.

His motto is "to baldly go where no man has bean before" and to that end he founded the New Millennium Bean Party, polling 122 votes in the 2001 general election. The 50-year-old Captain, who recently paid $750 to insure himself against alien abduction, plans to turn his apartment in Port Talbot, South Wales, into a bean museum. However, there is a downside to being Captain Beany. "I've been out of work since 1992," says Kirk, "because I've changed my name and dress up as Captain Beany... a job for a superhero is very hard to come by." Just don't let anyone call him a "has-bean!"

Bean Bathtub

Danny Cooper, a computer student from Kings Lynn, England, raised money for charity by immersing himself for two hours in a bathtub full of cold baked beans.

Captain Beany lives his life as a baked bean. The tomato sauce-soaked food gets his pulse racing so much that he regularly plunges into a bathtub full of them.

Bean Feats

In June 2004, Hollywood celebrated the 30th anniversary of the blockbuster movie Blazing Saddles, by producing a special edition DVD promotion. The event was happily celebrated at the Saddle Ranch Chop House in the heart of Hollywood and was marked with a human "bean dip" contest. Movie fans took turns to dive in and search through the beans for a Blazing Saddles DVD.

245

Ice-breakers

In a bid to boost sales, Japanese confectioners introduced an exciting new range of ice-creams in 2002. Customers could cool down with such exotic flavors as octopus, horseradish, shark's fin, garlic, potato and lettuce, whale, and cactus, not to mention basashi vanilla, which contained chunks of raw horse-flesh!

Chew it Over
Seattle's unlikeliest tourist attraction is the Gum Wall in Pike Place Market. The entire wall is covered in thousands of pieces of chewing-gum in all colors from the mouths of people from all over the world.

Breaking Bread
A church in Buffalo, New York, has decided that visitors should be able to grab lunch while worshiping. The True Bethel Baptist Church is the first in the U.S.A. to open its own Subway restaurant.

Champion Biscuit
The world's biggest ham biscuit was prepared at Smithfield, Virginia, in 2002. Made from 500 lb (230 kg) of ham, it measured a staggering 8 ft wide and 14 in (36 cm) tall.

Chickening Out

Kay Martin freaked out when the chicken she was cooking began to squawk. Steam had built up in the bird and was escaping through its vocal cords. Put off, Martin threw it out and hasn't cooked chicken since.

Don't Bug Me

Students at the Iowa State University Entomology Club don't just study six-legged bugs, they also eat them! Particular favorite accompaniments are a cajun sauce, covered in chocolate... or just dipped in Jell-O.

Gross Interest

Whereas most people like to pop chocolate into their mouth, John LaMedica prefers live cockroaches. The man known as "Jungle John" stuffed a record nine poisonous Madagascan cockroaches into his mouth at the same time during a Ripley's Believe It Or Not! TV show in 2003. John, from Newark, Delaware, admits his act is "really gross." He adds: "They hiss and have spikes on their legs that cut the inside of my mouth, and sometimes they defecate in your mouth, but you can't do much about it. It leaves a bitter taste."

Radiator Grill

Dave Curtis of Suffolk, England, converted his Skoda car into a wheely unusual barbecue!

Long-distance Call

When you visit a McDonald's drive-thru, no matter where you are, it's quite possible that your order is routed through a call center in Colorado Springs, Colorado. Within 30 seconds, the order you shout into the microphone is typed into a computer in Colorado and then routed back to that same McDonald's kitchen. The system apparently creates fewer errors.

Emergency Rations

A U.S. Army laboratory has developed a dried meal that can be hydrated with dirty water or, if absolutely necessary, a soldier's own urine. This is possible because a special membrane allows only water molecules to pass through and filters out more than 99 per cent of bacteria and most chemicals.

Gum Blondes

Artist Jason Kronenwald, from Toronto, Ontario, creates portraits of celebrities that appear to be made out of clay but are actually sculpted from chewing-gum. He doesn't like to chew gum himself, but instead persuades his friends to soften it up for his use. His Gum Blondes series includes singer Britney Spears and actress Pamela Anderson.

Having a Ball

Eric "Badlands" Booker, a 34-year-old 395-lb (180-kg) heavyweight has for the second year in a row, become the Matzo Ball Contest champ. In 2003, Booker earned a world record by wolfing down 21 of the baseball-size dumplings, which are made from meal, eggs, and chicken broth. In 2004, the subway operator gobbled up just 20 of the 5-oz (140-g) balls in the allotted 5 minutes 25 seconds, but still won. He prepared by eating 10 lb (4.5 kg) of cabbage three nights before the contest.

Dead as a Dodo

Benjie Moss, a student at Staffordshire University in England, created this life-sized sculpture of the long-extinct Dodo bird after he gave up smoking and started chewing gum to alleviate his cravings. Rather than discarding the gum, he put it to good use making this sculpture!

The Tipping Point

A 2003 survey of Domino's Pizza managers in the Washington D.C. area found that the day Saddam Hussein was captured, December 13, 2003, was the biggest day of the year for tips, and orders for meat-topped pies were the highest in two years.

To Diet For

Lacking willpower? Then "DDS," a new dental appliance, might help. The dental plate fits on the roof of the mouth and prevents people from shoveling in large quantities of food. One study has shown the $400 device helped people to lose more than 1 lb (0.5 kg) a week.

Wakey Wakey

A Minnesota dairy has begun producing milk that is spiked with caffeine. Called "Hyper Cow," the frothy breakfast staple contains as much caffeine and sugar as a can of soda.

A Colossal Appetite

In 1999, pizza-maker Jeff Parker, from Brooks in Alberta, Canada, came up with the world's biggest commercially available pizza. Called the "Colossal," it measures 3 ft (90 cm) wide and 4 ft (1.2 m) long, and serves 108 people.

My Head's Spinning

Now you can wash your dirty laundry in public and drink a cocktail at the same time! The Laundry Bar in Miami, Florida, is an ordinary laundromat but it also has a fully stocked and licensed bar.

Bean Feast

Tracy Ostmann loves to make jellybean art. She was once commissioned to create a jellybean painting of a great white shark for a Chicago aquarium. More recently, she produced a 15-color portrait of Martin Luther King Jr. While Ostmann loves her medium, she says she has to refrain from eating too many of the beans while working, just in case she makes herself sick.

Nutty Protester

To demonstrate his support for English culture and food, performance artist Mark McGowan decided to turn himself into a full English breakfast. For 12 days in November 2003, McGowan sat in a London shop window in a bath of baked beans, with two chips up his nose and 48 sausages wrapped around his head. Earlier in the year, he had protested against student debt by using his nose to roll a peanut along 7 mi (11 km) of London roads to the Prime Minister's front door at 10 Downing Street.

Speak for Yourself

Known as "Bread Head," Japanese artist Tatsumi Orimoto spent June 1996 strolling through London with baguettes tied to his head. Earlier, he had spent two years in Germany with a 9-ft (3-m) chimney in his backpack and five years with a cardboard box on his foot. He passed another year dragging an iron bath round New York's Greenwich Village. "It's my way of communicating," he says.

Vinegar Joes

Vinegar-lovers gather in South Dakota, for the annual Vinegar Festival. Top prize goes to the Mother of All Vinegars contest winner. There's also a tasting at the vinegar museum—sugar cubes are then supplied to freshen contestants' mouths.

Grow Your Own

Giles Peare, a farmer from West Sussex, in England, eats grubs, worms, and insects that he finds on his farm.

No Licking

The world's first—and only—hotel made entirely of salt has a "no licking" policy.

The Uyuni Salt Hotel is the only hotel in the world that is made entirely from salt.

Built on the world's largest salt bed, the Uyuni Salt Hotel is located west of Colchani, deep in the salt plains of Bolivia, South America. Passing the salt will never be a problem, as the salt will always be on the table—in fact, like everything else, the table is made of salt.

Even the hotel beds are made from salt crystals.

Super Cucumber

Willian H. Rainey, of Fort Worth, Texas, grew a cucumber to an amazing 4 ft 11 in (1.4 m)!

Sugar Sugar

Mary Horton is addicted to sugar—she eats an average of 2 lb (1 kg) of it every day!

Fungi Fun

Weighing over 21 lb (9.5 kg), this edible giant puffball fungus was discovered by A.B. Tyler near his home in New York.

A Big Fish

By swallowing 350 live minnows in under an hour, Shane Williams, of Wonder Lake, Chicago, smashed the existing record of 280, which had been set in 1998.

Naked Lunch?

At Germany's Bellview Restaurant the menus are painted on the bare skin of the waiters and waitresses.

On Ice

An 81-year-old Indian woman has eaten huge chunks of ice every day for the last 17 years to relieve stomach ache. Shanti Devi eats up to 22 lb (10 kg) of ice a day in the summer, and says she can't sleep without her daily ice intake, most of it from neighbors' refrigerators.

Pizza the Action

In August 1998, a company called Little Caesar's took an order from jeans manufacturer the VF Corporation of Greensboro, North Carolina, for 13,386 pizzas—to feed 40,160 employees at 180 locations in the U.S.A.

Stab in the Pack

A Michigan housewife was rushed to the hospital after accidentally stabbing herself with a shard of pasta. It entered her finger with such force that doctors had to remove part of her fingernail.

Shell Shock

Norwegian Rune Naeri swallowed 187 oysters in three minutes—more than one per second—at the 2003 Hillsborough Oyster Festival in Northern Ireland. His total almost doubled the previous world record.

Biting the Bullet

Eating a hot dog in May 2004, Californian Olivia Chanes bit on something hard. When she began complaining of a metallic taste in her mouth, doctors discovered that she had swallowed a 0.4 in (9 mm) bullet!

The Worms Turn

In November 2003, C. Manoharan swallowed 200 live earthworms in just 20 seconds on a beach in the Indian port of Chennai. Each worm was 4 in (10 cm) long, and it took him a year to prepare for the feat.

Sourpusses!

A St. Louis health commissioner has apologized to Mim Murray, 10, and Marisa Miller-Stockie, 12, after a city inspector shut down their lemonade stand for operating without a business license. The girls were just trying to raise money to buy laptop computers. The city later admitted that it was overzealous in its attempt to enforce its food and vendor permit rules.

Spam Cram

First held in 1978, Spamarama attracts thousands of Spamophiles to Austin, Texas, to an annual celebration of the famous tinned meat. Events include a Spam toss, a Spam-calling contest, and a Spam-eating competition, known as the "Spam Cram."

Eggstra Large

Take more than 5,000 eggs, add 50 lb (23 kg) of onions, 75 green bell peppers, 52 lb (24 kg) of butter, over 6 gal (23 l) of milk, 4 gal (15 l) of green onion tops, 2 gal (8 l) of parsley, some crawfish tails, and Tabasco pepper sauce to taste, and what have you got?... the Giant Omelette of Abbeville, Louisiana, which keeps on getting bigger each year. The Giant Omelette Celebration began in 1984 with 5,000 eggs. One egg has been added every year since.

Toe Sandwich

A 35-year-old Austrian man, hungry for a snack, hacked off the toes on his left foot, fried them, and ate them between two slices of bread—because he could find nothing else to eat! When ambulance staff arrived, the man offered a toe, saying it tasted like chicken!

Yellow Peril

Californian Ken Bannister, known as "Banana Man," has amassed more than 17,000 banana-related objects since he founded the International Banana Club in 1972. He has a banana-shaped putter and yellow golf balls; books on bananas; a banana-shaped couch; banana-related art, clothing, food, and toiletries; plus banana-shaped telephones, lamps, clocks, watches, soft toys, crockery, and cutlery!

Ice and a Slice?

This giant lemon grew in a hot house in Chippenham, England. Compared to this ordinary-sized lemon, it sure is a whopper!

When the Chips are Down

Nicknamed a "compulsive swallower," a man in the 1930s was reported to have swallowed several poker chips. This X-ray shows the chips inside the man's stomach.

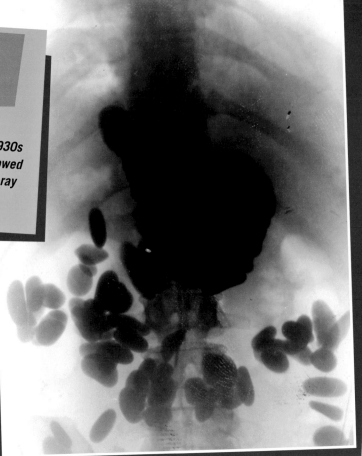

Eating Around the World

While he was rating the quality of diners around the world, Chicago food critic Fred E. Magel visited 46,000 restaurants in 60 countries over a period of 50 years.

There's the Grub

A Thai firefighter named Paisit Chanta thinks the key to a healthy life is to eat a live worm every single day. He has done so for 30 years and says that he has suffered nothing worse than mild flu.

Let Them Eat Cake

Drew Cerza, of Buffalo, New York, came up with a way to help others unload their unwanted holiday fruitcakes without tossing them in the trash. He asked for 100,000 cakes to be sent to him so that he could forward them to a food bank for the needy. His only stipulation was that the fruitcake be no more than two years old.

Double Trouble

An Israeli woman swallowed a fork in 2003 while trying to retrieve a cockroach from her throat. The insect jumped into her mouth while she was brushing her teeth, but when she tried to scoop it out with a fork, she swallowed that too.

It's No Turkey

Seattle soft drinks firm Jones Soda Co. introduced a turkey-and-gravy flavored fizzy drink for Christmas 2003. The novelty line proved to be so successful that it very quickly sold out, leaving thirsty customers clamoring for more.

Mouse Trap

In the 1940s, Dagmar Rothman performed a stunt at Ripley's New York City Odditorium in which he swallowed lemons and a mouse—and then regurgitated them.

Knit Wit

Eileen Mulrooney made a special kind of cake for her daughter's wedding. It looked yummy, but eating it wouldn't have been a pleasant experience—the whole cake was made from knitted wool!

Delivering the Goods

In 1998, Manhattan restaurant-owner Eddie Fishbaum was asked to deliver a plain pizza to TV host Eiji Bando in Tokyo, a distance of 6,753 mi (10,868 km). The pizza cost $7,000 including Eddie's airfare.

Brain Box

Etta's Lunch Box Café in Logan, Ohio, is decorated with owner Ladora Ouesley's collection of more than 400 lunchboxes. If customers point out the type of box they used to carry to school, Ladora can correctly identify the year they began their education.

Fowl Play

A two-hour jail riot, which resulted in an estimated $10,000-worth of damage, was sparked by the poor quality of a chicken dinner! Inmates at Autry State Prison in Pelham, Georgia, smashed lights, destroyed sprinkler heads, broke windows, and set fire to mattresses in December 2001 after one of the prisoners complained that his chicken was not thoroughly cooked.

Human Piggy Bank

When treated for stomach pains, a 62-year-old Frenchman was found to have swallowed 350 coins (francs and euros), plus assorted necklaces and needles. They weighed 12 lb (5 kg), as much as a bowling ball. The man, who died shortly afterward, had been swallowing coins for ten years despite his family's attempts to wean him off them.

Keen as Mustard

The first Saturday in August is Official Mustard Day in Mount Horeb, Wisconsin. Now in its 15th year, the celebration, held at the local mustard museum, features mustard tastings and a fiery cook-off.

Bite Size

Philadelphia confectioner Glenn Mueller Jr. has introduced a line of chocolate body parts. Enjoy the smooth texture of chocolate hearts, brains, lungs, and even dentures. If you can't resist one naughty bite, try the Mike Tyson special—a chocolate ear with a chunk missing!

Bean Cuisine

After taking part in a bean cook-off, contestants in the annual Bean Fest at Mountain View, Arkansas, then compete in an "outhouse race."

Choc Tactics

Tokyo chef Daisuke Nogami took one month and used 550 lb (250 kg) of white chocolate to create an 80-in (203-cm) tall replica of the *Venus de Milo* statue. It was displayed at the Food Art Museum in Tokyo in 2003.

Wonder Drugs

Inventor Ray Kurzweil, 56, takes 250 nutritional supplements a day. Why? He wants to live longer. Kurzweil believes that he is reprogramming his body to slow down the aging process. Maybe he's on to something: He claims that tests done by a Denver clinic show that his body resembles that of a man in his early forties.

Winging it

Ed "Cookie" Jarvis is a man of taste. In fact, the speed-eater from Long Island, New York, holds records for consuming such diverse items as ice-cream, pasta, pork ribs, corned beef, and cabbage. He has also eaten 91 Chinese dumplings in eight minutes, 40 meatballs in four minutes, and 2 lb (1 kg) of pickles in five minutes. He beat champion eater Sonya Thomas in a chicken-wing contest when he devoured 134 in just 12 minutes!

The Breakfast Club

Since 1990, Springfield, Massachusetts, has been home to the world's largest pancake breakfast, at which an 1,800-ft (549-m) long table seats more than 75,000 people. The feast requires 2,700 lb (1,225 kg) of flour, 600 lb (272 kg) of eggs, 210 lb (95 kg) of butter, and 210 gal (795 l) of water, all topped with 450 gal (1,703 l) of maple syrup. The pancakes are served with 3,370 gal (12,757 l) of coffee and 1,150 gal (4,353 l) of orange juice.

Choices, Choices

La Casa Gelato, in Vancouver, certainly knows ice-cream. The store offers customers nearly 500 flavors, although only 208 are available at any given time. Diversity in flavors apparently keeps customers coming back for more. The range includes such exotic tastes as curry, corn, durian, blue cheese, dandelion, garlic, vinegar, wasabi/green apple—and one that tastes like Guinness stout.

On the Double

On October 11, 2004, Domino's Pizza offered a free medium double crust pizza to any New Yorker who could prove that they had the same first and last name. Via an online search, Domino's estimated that there were at least 30 locals who would be able to take advantage of the offer.

Big Cheese

Sculptors Jimm Scannell and Jim Victor created a life-sized replica of a race car using about 3,500 lb (1,600 kg) of Cheddar cheese for the International Speedway in Richmond, Virginia.

Seedy Art

New York artist Hugh McMahon loves to create art with watermelons. Weighing up to 50 lb (23 kg), most pieces take him two hours to complete.

Eat My Shorts

When stopped by cops, an 18-year-old driver from Stettler, Alberta, tried to eat his own underwear in the hope that the cotton fabric would absorb the alcohol before he took a breathalyzer test. Maybe it worked, because his test level was below the legal limit and he was acquitted.

Melt Down

Originating at a campsite in Dorset, England, in 1997, cheese racing, as it's known, involves slices of processed cheese—still in their plastic

Whistle While You Work

In 1934, Paul Williams of Nashville, Tennessee, placed four golf balls in his mouth and managed to whistle at the same time!

wrapping—being thrown on to a hot barbecue by contestants. The cheese wrapper doesn't melt, and the first cheese slice to inflate, wins the cheese race!

Say Cheese!

Offbeat Canadian sculptor Cosimo Cavallaro doesn't work with ordinary art materials—he uses cheese! He has dressed a model from head to toe in cheese, sprayed jackets in cheese, and decorated a New York hotel room with dripping cheese. In 2001, he even painted an entire house in Wyoming with 10,000 lb (4,500 kg) of sprayed-on mozzarella. Then, in 2004, to prove that he could work with other materials, he covered a bed at a Manhattan hotel with slices of a 308-lb (140-kg) processed ham.

It's Electrifying

It was an illuminating experience for Russian Alvarez Kanichka when he swallowed live lightbulbs—and then retrieved them by pulling on the electrical cord, still attached!

Slippery Starter

Bored with beans on toast? Then, for a while, Edible, a restaurant in London, England, was the place to eat!

Created by Todd Dalton, from Louisiana, Edible offered cuisine for those with an open mind. As well as boiled rattlesnake, customers could try such delicacies as alligator stew and chocolate-covered scorpions. Sadly, Londoners' stomachs weren't up to the challenge, and Edible is now closed.

Chef Dan Craven boils rattlesnake to make a rattlesnake chili.

Tequila-flavored lollipops contain caterpillars or scorpions.

If you spy a fly in your soup, just count yourself lucky that you didn't order piranha fish and chips, or beer-battered locusts!

Fruity Heirloom

Some families pass down jewelry from generation to generation, but Margie Clark of Oklahoma, is giving her kids a shrivelled orange. The shrunken, rock-hard, nearly petrified piece of fruit has been in her family since 1921 when it was given to her father by his sister, it was then stored in a trunk.

Hot Favorite

Chicago-based Vienna Beef unveiled a 37-ft 2-in (11-m) long hot dog at the 2004 Taste of Chicago festival. The monster wiener was garnished with 1 gal (4 l) of mustard, 1 gal (4 l) of green relish, 140 tomato slices, 4 lb (2 kg) of chopped onions, and 70 pickle spears.

Cutting the Carbs

Jack LaLanne, 90, regarded by many as "the godfather of fitness," still works out for two hours a day, seven days a week. Ever since the age of 15, LaLanne has eaten a diet high in fruits and vegetables. Apparently, he hasn't had a sugary dessert since 1929.

Champion Chomper

Sonya Thomas, aged 36, of Alexandria, Virginia, joined the International Federation of Competitive Eating in only 2003, but the 105-lb (48-kg) rookie has already set records. These include eating 8.4 lb (3.8 kg) of baked beans in under three minutes, 167 chicken wings in 32 minutes, 11 lb (5 kg) of cheesecake in 9 minutes, 65 eggs in under 7 minutes, 38 lobsters in 12 minutes, and 432 oysters in 10 minutes.

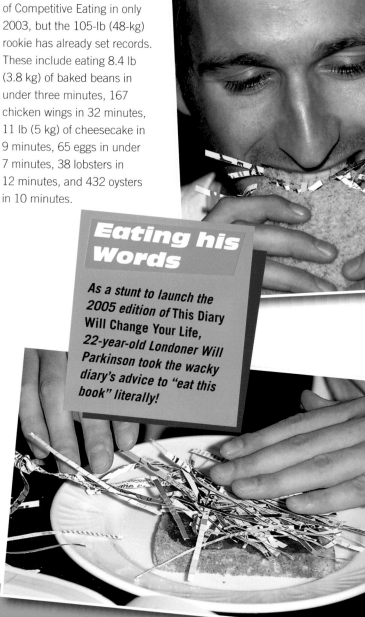

Eating his Words

As a stunt to launch the 2005 edition of This Diary Will Change Your Life, 22-year-old Londoner Will Parkinson took the wacky diary's advice to "eat this book" literally!

Helped by other ingredients, such as bread, jam, banana and vanilla milkshakes, beetroot, tomato ketchup, and Coke, Will successfully consumed the entire book in 7 hours!

Pumpkin Paddlers

An unusual contest is held annually in Nova Scotia, Canada—the pumpkin paddling regatta.

Every year, hundreds of water-loving gourd-enthusiasts compete in the race, which is held in the town of Windsor. A local pumpkin-grower, Howard Dill, raises a giant breed of pumpkin, called Giant Atlantic, and rather than wasting the hollowed-out flesh after selling the seeds, gives them to contestants of the regatta so that they can shape them to their own requirements.
Not only do contestants have to bring their own wetsuits in order to compete, they must also carve out the pumpkins' insides to create a cockpit.

Experienced pumpkin paddler Chip Peterson dons a helmet made out of a pumpkin.

The regatta organizers recommend that participants race in pumpkins that weigh more than 600 lb (272 kg).

Pride of Lions

During their annual pancake festival in 2002, members of the Lubbock Lions Club in Lubbock, Texas, made 30,724 pancakes in just eight hours.

Red Alert

Nicholas Huenefeld of Ohio can swallow 24 oz (680 g) of ketchup in one sitting.

Snail's Pace

A French seaweed collector retained one of the world's lesser-known sporting titles in August 2004—that of champion snail-spitter. Alain Jourden, aged 43, beat off 110 rivals from 14 different countries by propelling the live mollusk 30.8 ft (9.4 m) from a running start. However despite winning, he failed to match his own existing world record of 34.1 ft (10.4 m) because of some adverse wind conditions on the Brittany coast.

Carton Character

Anthony Key, from Bath, England, created a sculpture called Female Buddha using only chinese takeaway cartons!

Sausage Feat

A village in Northern Serbia displayed a 3,280-ft (1,000-m) long sausage during a traditional meat festival in 1997.

Pull Some Strings

Made using 18 gal (68 l) of olive oil, 1,100 lb (500 kg) of flour, and 1,800 eggs, this fettuccine took the record in Singapore in 1997 as the world's longest noodle. Forty chefs spent five days in the kitchen cooking up the record-breaking pasta. The hard work of the chefs and their assistants resulted in a staggering 3,776 ft (1,151 m) of the super strings!

273

What a Whopper

What is believed to be the world's biggest commercially available burger is on sale for $23.95 at Denny's Beer Barrel Pub in Clearfield, Pennsylvania. It weighs in at a mighty 6 lb (3 kg) and Denny's claim that no customer has ever managed to finish it.

Beef it Up

Clint Stephenson, an engineer from Texas, won the Sutter Home Wineries' 2004 Build a Better Burger Contest. His winner was a grilled California Avocado B.L.T. Burger with Caramelized Chipotle Onions and blue cheese spread. He plans to build a house with his $50,000 prize money.

A Cracking Idea

Competitors in the 4th of July sidewalk egg fry at Oatman, Arizona, cook eggs on the sidewalk using just the heat of the midday sun.

Internal Affairs

Donald Lerman lives up to his nickname of "The Beef." A stocky 5 ft 8 in (1.73 m) tall and weighing 185 lb (84 kg), in 2001 he broke the world burger speed-eating record by wolfing down 11 and a bit quarterpounders in 10 minutes. Donald prepares for eating competitions by drinking up to 1 gal (4 l) of water at a time.

Baker's Oven

Ivan "Chamouni" Chalbert baked more than bread in his 400°F (200°C) oven! The 19th century Russian baker could withstand the same heat that thoroughly cooked raw meat.

BAKER IRON WORKS LOS ANGELES

Ripley's

"CHAMOUNI" THE BAKER
EXHIBIT NO: 1106
COULD CLIMB INSIDE HIS OWN OVEN AT EXTREMELY HIGH TEMPERATURES

Totally

Obsessed

Buttery Burial

In "The Popcorn Sarcophagus," the renowned competitive eater, Crazy Legs Conti, was buried alive under 100 cu ft (3 cu m) of popcorn. Breathing through a custom-fitted snorkel as he ate, he used colored lights to signal—red meant "danger," green meant "OK," and yellow meant "alert, need more butter!"

To Cap it All

Over a period of 30 years, Emanuele "Litto" Damonte (1892–1985), the "Hubcap King" of Pope Valley, California, collected more than 2,000 vehicle hubcaps.

If the Hubcap Fits...

Sculptor Ptolemy Elrington of Brighton, England, recycles old hubcaps into sculptures, mostly of fish, "to try to say things about our wasteful society."

Foul Play

Eighty-three-year-old Abe Coleman of Tacoma, Washington, has a penchant for catching foul balls. For the past two decades, the sprightly octogenarian has stood in the parking lot of the town's minor-league ballpark during every game, complete with baseball glove in hand, running back and forth in hot pursuit of all those errant baseballs. When one really goes astray, he has even been known to crawl under parked cars to retrieve it.

Split Personality

England's Alfred West holds the world record for splitting hairs: He split a human hair into 18 parts, making all the cuts from one point.

Hubcap in Hand

Known as the "Hubcap Queen," Lucy Pearson of the U.S. has a collection of more than 200,000 hubcaps!

281

Great Ball of Paint

Every day since 1977, house painter Mike Carmichael of Alexandria, Indiana, has applied at least one coat of paint to a regulation baseball.

More than 20,500 coats of paint later, the initial 9-in (23-cm) circumference has ballooned to more than 104 in (264 cm), and the weight of the ball has increased to 2,200 lb (1,000 kg) making it the world's largest ball of paint. Mike lets a guest of honor paint every hundredth coat, and has kept detailed records of the many colors of the ball's layers. The ball has now grown so big that he has had to build a special room in his house just to store it. The attraction has drawn many visitors, some from as far away as Thailand.

Mike Carmichael accepts requests from total strangers to have a layer of the ball painted in their honor. He often paints their name or message on the ball.

Close to the Wire

"Clonia," created by Lyle Lynch of Phoenix, Arizona, was the biggest barbed-wire ball in the world from 1970 until the late 1990s. With a diameter of 80 in (2 m) and a weight of more than 5,000 lb (2,268 kg), it consists of 16 mi (26 km) of wire!

Let's Stick Together

Boys Town, Nebraska, is home to the world's largest ball of stamps. The ball, which weighs in at 600 lb (272 kg), is housed in the town's Philamatic Museum. It was pasted together by the local stamp-collecting club over the course of six months in the early 1950s. Why did the philatelists get so stuck in? "It must have been an exceptionally cold winter," says the museum's director.

First-class Effort

In the 1930s, postmaster Virden Graham of Indiana completed a 130-lb (59-kg) ball of brown cotton string that he had taken from first-class bundles. It took him 16 years, and the ball consisted of an impressive 78 mi (126 km) of string.

Stringing Us Along

For years Francis A. Johnson used to spend every lunch hour painstakingly wrapping twine on his farm in Darwin, Minnesota. When he died in 1989, the ball measured 12 ft (4 m) in diameter and weighed 17,400 lb (7,892 kg).

283

Stub it Out

Since 2001, anti-smoking activist Zhang Yue has attempted to convert China's 4 million smokers—one by one. Traveling around the country, he approaches smokers and tries to convince them to quit. He will even buy their cigarettes from them.

Swat Team

After a fly wrecked a lucrative deal by landing in a client's meal, Chinese businessman Hu Xilin vowed revenge. That was ten years ago and since then Hu says that he has killed 88 lb (40 kg) of flies and can identify 25 different species.

Habit-forming

Statistics compiled by the Obsessive Compulsive Foundation suggest that as many as one in 50 adults in the U.S.A. suffers from Obsessive Compulsive Disorder. These sufferers become obsessed by doubts or worries to the point where their lives become disrupted. They often feel compelled to perform certain actions—for example, repeated hand-washing, arranging, counting, collecting, and hoarding—in order to alleviate their distress.

The Little Top

Roll up for the smallest show on earth! Paul Tandy from Warwick, England, has spent the last nine years creating a model circus, with miniature animals, and more than 500 entertainers. Inspired by a visit to the circus when Paul was ten, P.J. Tandy's International Circus is accurate in every detail, down to a cannon, which fires a mini human cannon ball, and tiny elephant droppings.

Cartoon Capers

George C. Reiger Jr. (far right), a postal worker from Pennsylvania and his father George Reiger (right), are goofy about Disney characters.

The 51-year-old Reiger Jr. has more than 1,650 Disney tattoos from the base of his neck to the tops of his toes. His first cartoon tattoo was Mickey Mouse on his forearm. Now the whale from *Pinocchio* (U.S. 1940) yawns on his belly, Beauty and the Beast dance on his left shoulder, and Alice in Wonderland fills his upper arm. On his back are 103 Dalmatians—his tattoo artist got carried away! George spends $50,000 a year on his Disney habit and has even spent all six of his honeymoons at Disney World in Florida.

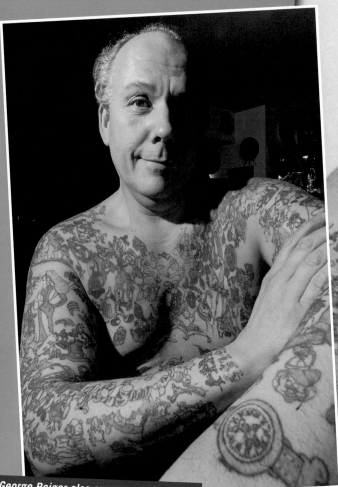

George Reiger also owns more than 19,500 Disney collectibles and lives in a custom-built, Disney-themed house.

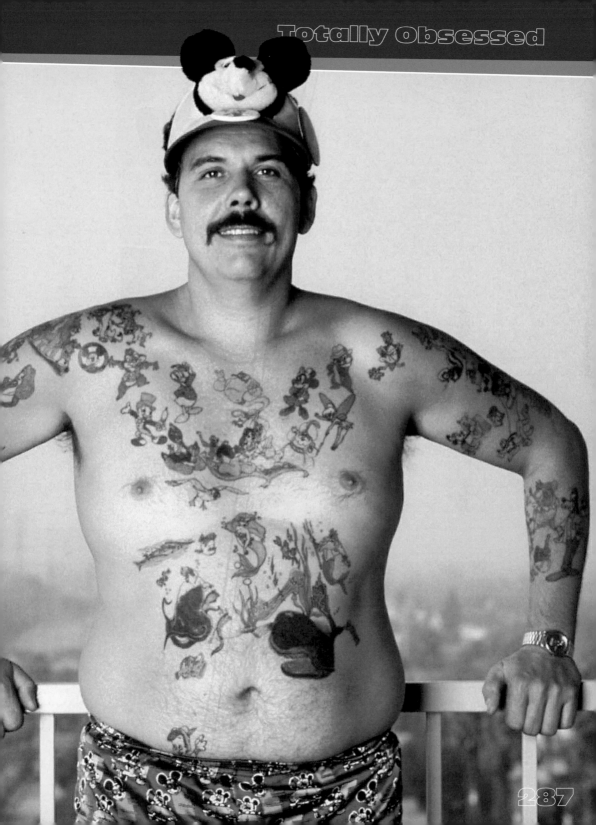

All Mixed Up

An Englishman who gave up trainspotting as it was too boring now has more than 1,000 pictures of cement-mixers. Ronnie Crossland, of Yorkshire, first developed his passion after spotting a new mixer being delivered to a building site in 1987. He has since traveled more than 200,000 mi (322,000 km) taking photos of cement-mixers, which he describes as "things of incredible beauty."

Skater Mom

Barbara Odanaka can't seem to outgrow her childhood obsession with skateboarding. When she isn't skating around her house in Orange County, California, she is busy running the International Society of Skateboarding Moms, or using her skateboard to distribute books to needy children, or promoting her book, which is titled… you guessed it, Skateboard Mom.

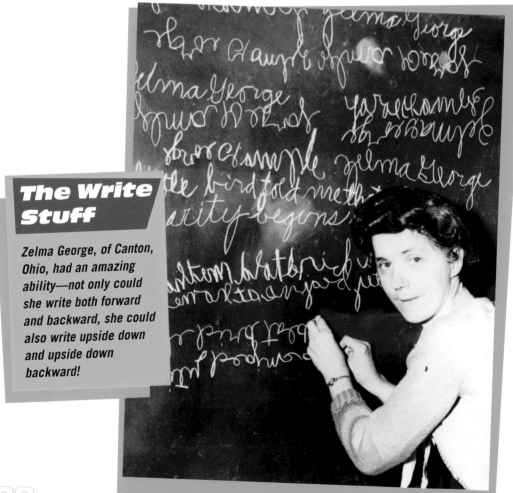

The Write Stuff

Zelma George, of Canton, Ohio, had an amazing ability—not only could she write both forward and backward, she could also write upside down and upside down backward!

Double-blind Test

Frank Keith of Illinois, could write backward, upside-down, and blindfolded! He could also simultaneously write any name or phrase with his left hand in front and his right hand behind.

Praise the Gourd

Marvin Johnson could never get enough gourds. He and his wife Mary had so many of the strange-looking vegetables at their house in Angier, North Carolina, that they set up a Gourd Museum in 1965. The exhibits are mostly of gourd art. There is a gourd xylophone, a gourd Popeye, and a menagerie of gourd animals. "I've made lots of friends through gourds," Marvin once said.

Get Set, Go

Jane Withers, a child star of Hollywood films of the 1930s and 1940s, has a collection of showbiz memorabilia large enough to fill a warehouse. Jane's stash of more than 42,000 items includes parts of TV and movie sets, costumes, dolls, and scripts.

The Best Possible Paste

Dr. Valkopolkov, of Saginaw, Michigan, has collected more than 800 tubes of toothpaste from around the world, including such exotic flavors as tuna and Scotch.

The Hole Story

The world's most pierced woman, Brazilian Elaine Davidson, puts her finger through her pierced tongue! So far she has 1,903 body piercings. Elaine has also been known to walk on beds of fire, broken glass, and nails. For her next feat: She wants to exceed 2,000 piercings!

Living Doll

A Maryland couple have raised a Cabbage Patch doll as their only son for 19 years. Pat and Joe Posey treat the 1-ft (0.3-m) doll, christened Kevin, as a human. He "speaks" through Joe, has his own 1,000-sq-ft (93-sq-m) playroom at the couple's home, a full wardrobe, and $4,000 of savings for when he goes to college!

Flip-flop Fiend

Since 1996, Russell Doig has gathered more than 4,000 flip-flops from his local beach near Townsville, Queensland, Australia. Doig combs Alva beach every weekend, scooping up washed-up flip-flops with a special spike before nailing them to his back fence.

In a Spin

In April 2004, hula hoop performer Alesya Goulevich spun 100 hula hoops simultaneously, at the Big Apple Circus, Boston.

A Sick Sense of Humor

Steve Dixon has been collecting airline sick-bags for 23 years. In that time he has amassed a collection of more than 180 bags.

Is it a Bird, is it a Plane...

Californian John Ninomiya is one of only a few cluster balloonists in the world. He and his crew tie between 50 and 150 latex balloons on to a harness... and up and away he goes. So far, he has made about two dozen balloon flights.

Duck and Cover

Nancy Townsend is so obsessed with her pet ducks and geese that she has invented diapers for them so that they can live indoors. Nancy dresses as Mother Goose, and is often seen taking her birds for walks on a leash.

Mac Attack

Computer technician Andrew Dusing makes furniture out of old Macintosh computer boxes and their Styrofoam inserts. His New York apartment is furnished with his recycled creations: A sofa, a dining table, a set of chairs, and CD racks. His ambition is to one day make a '57 Chevy.

Blood Brothers

Grab a bite with local vampires on International Vampire Meetup Day. Once a month, thousands of aspiring bloodsuckers meet at an appointed time in more than 650 different locations around the world. The most popular cities for meetups are: London, followed by New York City, and Houston, Texas.

Big Breakfast

Frank Staley has collected more than 400 breakfast cereal boxes. This is 400 too many for his wife, who has ordered him to move some of them out of their Ohio home.

Hearse Case Scenario

Rachel Ellam-Lloyd was so obsessed with vampires that she used to drive her young daughter to school in London in a 23-ft (7-m) long hearse. Little Georgina sat in the back where the coffin should be. Rachel also used the hearse—bought for her by her husband—to go shopping and to attend meetings of the Vampire Connections group.

Beam Me Up

Star Trek fans Mikel and Craig Salsgiver displayed the Vulcan greeting as they renewed their marriage vows on the Starship Enterprise.

The Salsgivers were among four couples to be selected to take part in the "Intergalactic Weddings" package, offered by the Las Vegas Hilton's "Startrek: The Experience" attraction. The vows, which were taken on the couple's fifth wedding anniversary, were made on the bridge of the Starship Enterprise.

Spaced Out

1 Orlando, Florida, dentist Denis Bourguignon and his entire staff wear Star Trek uniforms while working on patients

2 Britain's David Nutley is so obsessed with Star Wars that he's made his own version. He filmed Dark Skies in his spare room and nearby woods for $900

3 Star Trek fan Barbara Adams of Little Rock, Arkansas, wears her Starfleet Commanding Officer's uniform everywhere she goes— even on jury duty

4 British Trekkie Tony Alleyne has turned his flat into a replica of the Starship Enterprise

5 Star Trek fan Daryl Frazetti from Boston, Massachusetts, dressed his cat Bones in a Dr. McCoy uniform

Mikel Salsgiver made all the outfits for her Trekkie wedding party.

Holy Roller

"Rolling saint" Lotan Baba makes holy pilgrimages through the Indian countryside by lying on the ground and rolling sideways to his destination. In 1995, he rolled nearly 2,500 mi (4,023 km), averaging between 6 mi (10 km) and 13 mi (21 km) a day. He embarked on a 1,500-mi (2,414-km) roll from India to Pakistan in 2003.

Log Jam

The front yards of Bynum, North Carolina, are adorned with wooden figures of dogs, elephants, giraffes, and other animals. They are the work of Clyde Jones who, for more than 20 years, has used his chainsaw to carve out distinctive critters from log stumps. Dozens of his creations stand outside his own house, which was covered in penguins.

Fowl Play

Armando Parra is a professional chicken-catcher in Key West, Florida, where an estimated 2,000 of the fast-breeding birds run loose in the streets. Armando catches the chickens unharmed, and then they are sent to live on a farm.

She Ain't Heavy

An Indian man is carrying his elderly mother on a 17-year-long pilgrimage from their home in northern India to Bangalore in the south. Kailashgiri Brahmachari carries his blind mother in a basket on one shoulder and, in another basket, their belongings. By walking a

How the West was Washed

Slater Barron, of Long Beach, California, collects lint from her own laundry, and from that of neighbors and friends, and stores it in color-coded boxes in her studio/garage. She then uses the lint to make pictures of all kinds of people and objects, including this portrait of actor John Wayne, which can be seen in the Ripley's Museum in Hollywood.

couple of miles each day, he hopes to reach their destination in 2013.

Captain Cutlass

As his alter ego, Captain Cutlass, Adrian Collins from Kent, England, organizes and competes in the annual World Plank Walking Championship, held on the Isle of Sheppey. Plankers come from all over the world to take part.

Ripley's

ART MADE OUT OF LIINT
EXHIBIT NO: 13998
THIS LINT ARTWORK OF JOHN WAYNE IS ACTUALLY LIFE-SIZE, AT 6 FT 4 IN (2 M)

Royal Flush

Australian Janet Williams is such a fan of the British monarchy that she has "royalty rooms" in her home in Sydney, dedicated to her collection of royal memorabilia.

Slap Dash

After years of frustration at finding grammatical errors in newspapers, Jeff Rubin, who runs a newsletter production business, created a new holiday: National Punctuation Day. He hopes that the holiday, which is celebrated every year on August 22, will bring some attention to the widespread problem of poor punctuation.

Full of Beans

In the 1990s, Peggy Gallagher left her job as a paralegal in Chicago to pursue her obsession with Beanie Baby toys. She tracked down rare ones, wrote a book about them, and became a Beanie Baby authenticator—someone who decides whether or not Beanies are genuine.

Watching You

During one series of TV's Big Brother, Gillian Dutfield, of Shropshire, England, lived her life according to the housemates. She cooked the same meals as them, and ate and slept at the same time as them. She even shaved her pet dog with the message to the audience, "Vote for Brian!"

Gnome Home

More than 2,000 garden gnomes and pixies roam free at Ann Atkin's gnome sanctuary in Devon, England. Ann, who is 67, founded the International Gnome Club in 1978. She stoutly defends her lengthy garden-gnome fixation by saying, "I think people form an affinity with them."

The Bottom Line

Over the past 30 years, Barney Smith has painted more than 600 toilet seats. He displays his unusual collection in his garage in Alamo Heights, Texas.

Grand Slam

Jason Alan Pfaff of Ohio is a man on a mission: To visit every single Denny's restaurant in the world. His website contains reviews of the 200 or more locations he has visited.

The Winner by a Nose

Ashrita Furman of New York holds the most world records of any individual, including titles for pogo-stick jumping, brick-carrying, underwater rope-jumping, and sack-racing. In New York in 2004, he also succeeded in pushing an orange for 1 mi (1.6 km) in a time of 24 minutes 36 seconds, using his nose!

299

The School Run

Author and athlete Sri Chinmoy sponsored a curious endurance race in New York City in 1998. The 3,100-mi (4,989-km) course consisted of running round and round a Queens school between 6 a.m. and midnight for weeks on end. The leading runners completed, on average some 115 laps of the school each day. The winner, Hungary's Istvan Sipos, finished the course in 47 days.

Surf's Up

On February 29, 1976, Dale Webster pledged to surf off the coast of California every day until Leap Day fell again on the fifth Sunday of February. That meant 28 years, or more than 10,000 days of surfing, before he stopped in 2004. He postponed his wedding for ten years, never took a vacation, and took poorly-paid night jobs so that he would be free for surfing during the day.

Stuck on You

Art student Jillian Logue, of Florida, made this senior prom dress and tuxedo entirely out of colored duct tape!

Wash Day Blues?

No stranger to the Ripley's Believe It or Not! TV show, Kevin Thackwell, has broken records by attaching 120 clothes pins to his face and neck. Kevin, who is also known as the "Clothes Pin Man," clearly isn't worried about wrinkles.

LKING
ACKWARDS
AROUND
HE WORLD

ALKED EVERY
TEP BACKWARD
CROSS THE
NITED STATES
ND CONTINENTAL
UROPE

VAS BARRED
Y ASIA MINOR
OVERNMENT
ROM WALKING
ACROSS ASIA
MINOR COUNTRY

STARTED
4-15-1931
FINISHED
10-24-1932

MY RECORD
NONSTOP WALK
45 MILES IN
12 AND ½ hr.

DONT MISS READING THE BOOK OF
AROUND THE WORLD BACKWARDS

Don't Look Back

During the 1930s, Plennie Wingo walked backward around the world! Later he walked backward from LA to San Francisco as part of a Ripley's museum promotion. He always wore mirrored glasses so that he could see where he was going.

Completely Cuckoo

With 561 cuckoo-clocks, Roman Piekarski, proprietor of the Cuckooland Museum in Cheshire, England, has the largest collection of cuckoo-clocks in the world. He dreads Daylight Saving Time, for twice a year it takes him around 12 hours altogether to change all his clocks!

White Spirit

In January 2005, 82-year-old Paul Schipper clocked up an incredible 3,903 consecutive days' skiing on Sugarloaf Mountain in Maine, despite the fact that he is almost blind in one eye. From 1981 to 2005, the senior citizen went out skiing every single day that the mountain was open.

Reverse Gear

India's Samir Tandon can sing songs, read newspapers, and repeat entire conversations backward.

Casket Case

Casket carver Mark Zeabin from Krestova, British Columbia, makes a line of furniture that will last a lifetime—and then some. For Mark is so keen on coffins that he has designed stereo stands, bars, and even sofa beds that will convert into coffins upon the owner's demise. His theory is that it's a false economy to buy a bookshelf that stores only books when you can have one that will eventually store you too.

Tomb Raider

Sara Lock from Suffolk, England, was so enthralled by Ancient Egyptian culture that she turned her spare room into an Egyptian tomb.

Christmas Crackers!

Some folk wish it could be Christmas every day—and for Andy Park it is! Since 1991, Andy, of Wiltshire, England, has been celebrating Christmas on a daily basis.

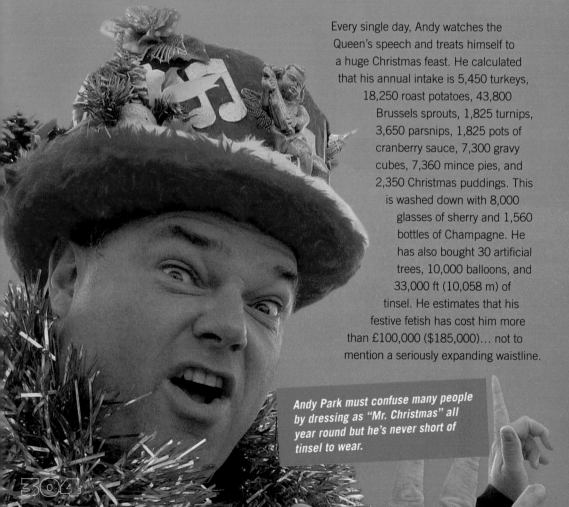

Every single day, Andy watches the Queen's speech and treats himself to a huge Christmas feast. He calculated that his annual intake is 5,450 turkeys, 18,250 roast potatoes, 43,800 Brussels sprouts, 1,825 turnips, 3,650 parsnips, 1,825 pots of cranberry sauce, 7,300 gravy cubes, 7,360 mince pies, and 2,350 Christmas puddings. This is washed down with 8,000 glasses of sherry and 1,560 bottles of Champagne. He has also bought 30 artificial trees, 10,000 balloons, and 33,000 ft (10,058 m) of tinsel. He estimates that his festive fetish has cost him more than £100,000 ($185,000)… not to mention a seriously expanding waistline.

Andy Park must confuse many people by dressing as "Mr. Christmas" all year round but he's never short of tinsel to wear.

Santa's Little Helpers

Alex Adlam's house in Cheltenham, England, is full of hundreds of Santas in all shapes and sizes. Alex is unable to resist any item of Christmas memorabilia, from snowmen and reindeer, to stockings and elves. His collection of ornaments, plates, cushions, and decorations has turned his home into a grotto.

Running on Empties

David Pimm has a collection of more than 10,000 different milk bottles at his home on the Isle of Wight, England.

Soil Baron

This U.S. soil collector gathered soil from every single U.S. state. He kept each sample in a small container attached to a map on the spot where it came from.

He's a Barbie Boy

Tony Mattia of Brighton, England, owns more than 1,100 Barbie dolls. He started collecting them in the 1960s. "My parents bought me an Action Man," he says, "but I dressed him up in Barbie's clothes." A Barbie that he bought for £1 ($2) in 1962 is now worth at least £200 ($400). Tony changes the costume of every doll he owns once a month.

Navel Gazing

Every day since 1984, Graham Barker from Perth, Australia, has been collecting fluff from his navel. He now has 0.54 oz (16.8 g), which is the world's largest collection.

In for a Penny...

Arizona's Steve Baker is crazy about pennies. He makes skirts, shirts, and bathing suits out of the coins, but his pride and joy is his jumpsuit made out of no fewer than 3,568 of them. It took him 800 hours to make and it weighs 32 lb (15 kg). Just in case anyone has any doubt as to Steve's obsession, he also drives around in a van covered in 90,000 pennies.

Bottle Neck

Indian artist Mayapandi has been painting figures on the insides of bottles for the past six years and hopes eventually to fit 500 figures in one bottle.

Sweet on Pez

"They're fun, they're cute, they're small," says Gary Doss, creator of the Burlingame Museum of Pez Memorabilia in California. He's describing Pez candy dispensers—and Gary should certainly know. For, since starting his collection in 1988, he has amassed hundreds of different dispensers, including ones with character heads of Mary Poppins, Mickey Mouse, Batman, and Santa Claus.

Overexposed

Photographer Spencer Tunick is driven by the urge to photograph masses of nude bodies in public places. He favors famous locations, such as New York City's Grand Central Station. Since 1992, he has staged his work on every continent, using up to 7,000 volunteers at once.

The King and I

Paul MacLeod claims to be Elvis' number one fan—he even called his son Elvis Aaron Presley MacLeod. On show at Graceland Too, his house in Holly Springs, Mississippi, are Elvis' 1951 report card, a gold lamé suit supposedly worn by the King for a concert in 1957, and a casket that plays "Return to Sender," in which Paul plans to be buried.

A Colorful Life

Just as actor Yul Brynner wore only black for 45 years, so Jean Rath of Santa Maria, California, is obsessed with purple.

She has lilac hair, wears purple clothes, drives only purple cars (with "I Love Purple" bumper stickers), and her business cards and checks name her as "The Purple Lady." She lives in a lavender house, with a lavender mailbox and fence. Of course everything inside is purple too—her violet toilet paper has to be ordered from Canada. Her late husband Bill also wore purple.

Everything in Jean Rath's house has to be purple—unable to buy a refrigerator or dishwasher in her favorite color, she simply painted them purple.

It's not difficult to see why British folk musician Cresby Brown is known as "Mr Red." He dresses from head to foot in bright scarlet and owns a wealth of red accessories.

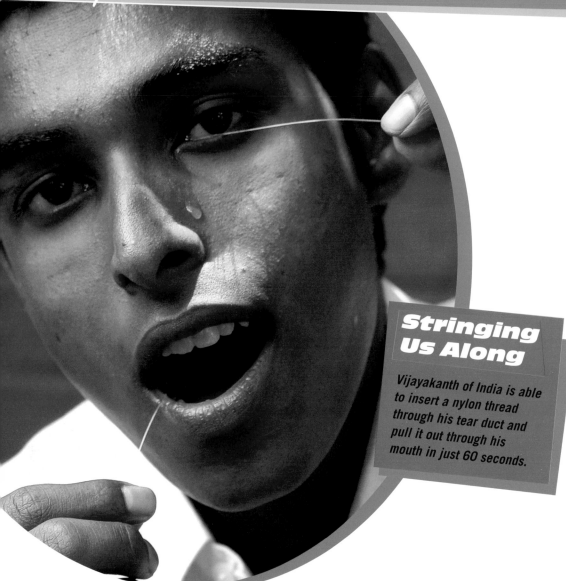

Stringing Us Along

Vijayakanth of India is able to insert a nylon thread through his tear duct and pull it out through his mouth in just 60 seconds.

Shock Treatment
A holy man in northern India touches live electricity wires every day—for kicks. Sadhu Mangal Das, aka "Current Baba," touches a naked wire at least three times a day.

In the Can
Richard Sangster, from the Netherlands, began collecting soft-drinks cans in 1983 and now has more than 10,000, including a German series of Backstreet Boys Pepsi cans.

Book Him!
In 2001, police drove 120 mi (190 km) to LeRoy Anderson's home in Mapleton, Minnesota, brandishing an arrest warrant—because he had forgotten to return two overdue library books.

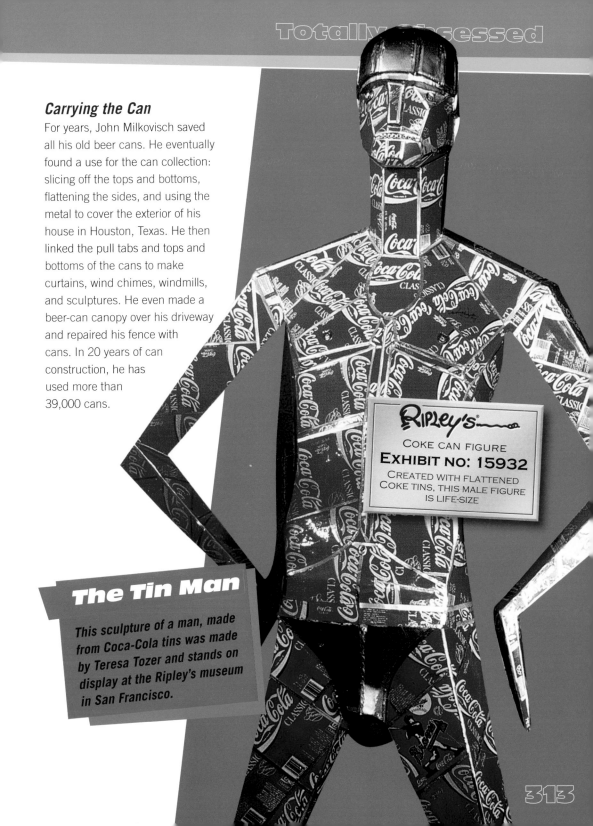

Carrying the Can

For years, John Milkovisch saved all his old beer cans. He eventually found a use for the can collection: slicing off the tops and bottoms, flattening the sides, and using the metal to cover the exterior of his house in Houston, Texas. He then linked the pull tabs and tops and bottoms of the cans to make curtains, wind chimes, windmills, and sculptures. He even made a beer-can canopy over his driveway and repaired his fence with cans. In 20 years of can construction, he has used more than 39,000 cans.

The Tin Man

This sculpture of a man, made from Coca-Cola tins was made by Teresa Tozer and stands on display at the Ripley's museum in San Francisco.

RIPLEY's

COKE CAN FIGURE

EXHIBIT NO: 15932

CREATED WITH FLATTENED COKE TINS, THIS MALE FIGURE IS LIFE-SIZE

Read All About It

Artist Ronald Max Vollmer produced a unique maze constructed from more than 50,000 old books! Visitors to the maze could wind their way through passages constructed from books stacked high upon one another. Not only could visitors view the piece, but they could also leave their own mark on the installation, by adding their own books if they wished to.

Concrete Proof

Benedictine monk Joseph Zoettel dedicated his life to constructing models of religious landmarks. He spent 50 years making miniature versions of buildings such as the Colosseum and the Vatican. Brother Joseph died in 1961, but 125 of his concrete reproductions are still exhibited at the Ave Maria Grotto at Cullman, Alabama.

Going by the Wayside

Over a period of 14 years, Fred Smith, a retired lumberjack from Phillips, Wisconsin, sculpted a cast of bizarre characters in concrete. More than 200 of his figures— including cowboys, miners, soldiers, and various animals—still stand by the wayside, and many of them are decorated with beer bottles from Smith's own tavern.

Vintage Fashion

German fashion designer Josefine Edle von Krepl has spent her life collecting old clothes. She has hoarded more than 3,000 garbage-can bags full of used garments, many of them date back to the 1920s, because she could never bear to throw anything away.

Bus Fair

Geoff Price, of Walsall, England, has spent the past 44 years collecting toy buses. He has nearly 8,000 models from around the world, and his hobby takes up so much space that he and his wife have been forced to move to a bigger house three times.

Island of the Dolls

For 50 years, Julian Santana scoured the garbage dumps of Mexico City. He was looking for discarded dolls, which he then hung from trees on an island

Beyond the Grave

Los Angeles is home to the Virtual Pet Cemetery for Tamagotchis, where bereaved children can go to pay their last respects to their dearly departed virtual friends.

in the city's Teshuilo Lake, where he lived alone. He collected thousands of dolls altogether, helped by locals who would take boats to the island and exchange old dolls for the vegetables he grew.

Gone to Pot

The Portable Border installation consisted of 100 plant pots in a line, which stretched as far as 40 ft (12 m). That wasn't all there was to this piece of art, because the flowery line moved approximately 2.5 mi (4 km) through the streets of London, England, during April 2004! British artist Phil Coy simply took the plant at the back of the line and moved it to the front, then took the next plant at the back and moved that to the front, and so on until he eventually reached his destination!

Buzz Off

In 1998, Californian Mark Biancaniello was covered in an estimated 350,000 bees, which weighed a total of 87.5 lb (40 kg).

Magnetic Personality

Over the past 30 years, Louise J. Greenfarb, of Las Vegas, Nevada, has collected more than 29,000 refrigerator magnets, including some featuring portraits of sports heroes, cartoon characters, and presidents. Her wish is to be buried in her refrigerator, surrounded by a thousand of her favorite magnets.

In at the Deep End

A Chinese pensioner called Yan performs a daily exercise of walking backward around Bayi Lake because he believes it is good for his health. Unfortunately, in April 2003 he was so busy counting his steps that he lost his bearings, fell in, and had to be rescued by fellow walkers.

Every Night at the Movies

Derek Atkins, of York, England, has visited Odeon cinemas eight times a week since 1988. But he doesn't go to watch the movies—he goes to study the décor. Derek, who used to work for Odeon as an usher and projectionist, admits he is obsessed with the Odeon chain. "If I can't see a film at the Odeon, I won't go to see the film at all," he says.

Dear Diary...

For no less than four hours a day, every day, from 1972 to 1996, Robert Shields, of Dayton, Washington, typed out a record of absolutely everything that happened

to him. His diary, which at 38 million words is thought to be the world's longest, is stored in more than 80 cardboard boxes. An example of his attention to detail is: "July 25, 1993, 7 a.m.: I cleaned out the tub and scraped my feet with my fingernails to remove layers of dead skin."

A Perfect Match

Prateep Tangkanchanawelekul, from Thailand, has an amazing collection of more than 100,000 matchboxes, including some rare ones. He has even made a jacket out of some of the matchboxes in his collection and claims to wear it wherever he goes.

The Long Way Home

In 2002, a Japanese canoeist finished a whopping 5,965-mi (9,600-km) journey around the country's coast… 23 years after he started! Reiji Yoshioka began his adventure in 1979 from near his home in Kanagawa, and always fitted it in with his work as a printer. He was 64 when he completed the final leg of his trip, which was around the northern Japanese island of Hokkaido.

Salad Days

Radish fanatics can celebrate their devotion to this underrated vegetable every December 23 at the Night of the Radishes exhibition in Oaxaca, Mexico. Huge radishes are carved into highly detailed figures and displayed in intricate scenes that reflect the local culture.

Trunk Call

Ever since receiving his first ornamental elephant as a gift from his sister-in-law on his wedding day in 1967, Ed Gotwalt has had a thing about pachyderms. His collection soon grew and his wife suggested he open a museum. Today, Mr. Ed's Elephant Museum in Orrtanna, Pennsylvania, is home to more than 6,000 elephants made from just about every known substance. In his spare time, Ed tours the country selling elephants' favorite food—peanuts!

That Really Sucks

California-based production artist Charlie Lester has been obsessed with vacuum cleaners since early childhood. He has acquired about 140 vintage vacuums (dating from 1905 to 1960) in the past four decades, and is an active member of the Vacuum Cleaner Collectors Club.

Well Done

Nearly 20 years ago, Deborah Henson-Conant got distracted and left a pot of cider on the stove for too long, and was fascinated by the result. Inspired, she decided to create the Burnt Food Museum to showcase all of her culinary disasters. Unfortunately, the museum, which is located in Arlington, Massachusetts, had to be temporarily closed in 2004—owing to fire damage.

Do You Take this Superman?

Marcella Encinas was convinced that her husband-to-be, actor Scott Cranford, was her real-life Superman. Therefore, when the couple were looking for a suitable wedding venue in June 2001, they chose Metropolis, Illinois, the self-styled home of Superman, and arranged for Scott to attend the ceremony dressed in full Superman costume. Wonder Woman was the matron of honor, and Robin, Batman's sidekick, was the best man. Among the guests was a dog wearing a superhero cape!

Word Perfect

An Indian man has memorized the entire Oxford Advanced Learners' Dictionary. It took Mahaveer Jain just ten months to remember each of the 80,000 individual entries. He can also recall their exact sequence and the page on which they appear.

Beatlemania

Beatle-mad Argentinean Rodolfo Vazquez keeps more than 5,600 items of Fab Four memorabilia in his loft. Among his most treasured possessions are some bricks from the Cavern Club in Liverpool, England, where the Beatles first played.

Venerable Beads

Over a period of 13 months, working eight hours a day, Faris Hassan, of Amman, Jordan, used more than 175,000 beads to make a 23-ft (7-m) long rosary.

Roll with the Punches!

At 50 years old, fitness instructor Ken Richmond appeared on the Ripley's TV show as the Human Cannon Ball.

Sparks fly as the gun is fired!

Ken tenses before the cannon ball is fired at him.

His shows of death-defying strength involved having a cannon ball dropped on his head, a wrecking ball smashed into his stomach, and a cannon ball fired at his stomach. He must have a six-pack of steel!

Ken Richmond gathers his strength for the challenge.

Smoke billows out and Ken stays tensed and stationary as the ball flies at him!

He begins to double-up as the ball impacts.

Thrown back by the impact and…

…backward he goes into the straw bales!

Tread Carefully

A couple in Helena, Montana, have built their home mainly out of tires and aluminum drinks cans. While 250 used car tires form the basic structure of the building, the interior is decorated with more than 13,000 cans. Among the peculiar sculptures is a buffalo made from chicken wire and beer bottles.

What's the Score?

Experimental Chilean artist Antonio Becerro devised a novel way of creating a painting in 2003. Dressed all in white, Becerro stood in front of a huge white canvas "goal," while top soccer player Francisco Huaiquipan took shots with a freshly painted football. Each time Huaiquipan hit the target, the painting received another splash of color from the ball.

Take a Gander at this Goose

There's a bird's eye view from every single room of one house in Hazard, Kentucky. For the house, built in the 1940s by John Stacy, is shaped just like a giant goose, with the head and neck protruding from the roof. The home even has egg-shaped windows.

Wishing Well

Royal College of Art student Kate MccGwire created "Brood" out of 22,000 chicken wishbones. The piece was displayed as part of her 2004 degree exhibition in London.

325

Backward Looking

Lorrain Chevalier, of Philadelphia, Pennsylvania, seen here in 1937, was actually able to sit on her own head! The Chevalier family claims that in 200 years only one person in each generation possessed such dexterity.

Animal Magic

Snowy Farr, of Cambridge, England, is so fond of white mice that he often slips the head of a live one into his mouth! It's all for a good cause though—Snowy has raised more than £60,000 ($120,000) for charity over the past 25 years.

Hidden Treasures

In 2003, Corinne Turner of Layton, Utah, bought a 99 cent wallpaper roll at a liquidation store and was stunned to find it hid five paintings by Italian artist Pino Daeni. Turner sold the paintings, which were valued

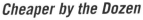

at $6,000, and donated a portion of the revenue to the Multiple Sclerosis Society. Daeni was so inspired by Turner's actions that he contributed 21 more paintings.

Cheaper by the Dozen

When Bob Memmot and Corinne Hanks, of Mapleton, Utah, married in June 2003, they significantly increased their family size: together they have a staggering 26 children, ranging in age from 13 to 34—and 34 grandchildren.

Hippo Crates

Visitors to Hutto, Texas, can't fail to notice that the town is swarming with hippos. There were around 100 at the last count, all arriving in crates on the orders of Mayor Mike Fowler as part of his drive to

promote the community. Most of the concrete beasts stand nearly 3 ft (1 m) tall and weigh more than 700 lb (317 kg), but Fowler has plans for a 20 ft (6 m) model—the biggest in the world.

Holy Smoke

Dharmendra Singh, of Bikaner, India, chain-smokes—through his ears! Dharmendra, who had always wanted to do something different, can smoke up to 20 cigarettes in a row in this bizarre fashion. He can also whistle through his nose.

327

Eye of the Needle

An English artist is the creator of some minuscule works of art—some of them are even tiny enough to fit inside the eye of a needle!

An amazing feat—a scene including a house, trees, and greenery carved on the head of a pin!

Snow White and the Seven Dwarfs.

Willard Wigan, 48, from Birmingham, England, makes his miniature sculptures under a microscope, employing shards of glass to cut his materials and using his own eyelashes as a paintbrush. Each sculpture takes around four months to complete. Among his fantastic works are a model of the Statue of Liberty, so tiny that it fits inside the eye of a needle; Snow White and the Seven Dwarfs, who also sit in the eye of a needle; a golden ship on a speck of crystal; a polar bear standing on a grain of sugar; a mini man wrestling with a life-sized ant; a re-creation of French sculptor Auguste Rodin's "The Thinker" on a pin head; and a figure of the biblical character Samson inside a human hair!

The Statue of Liberty carved inside the eye of a needle.

Child's Play

An ordinary child's kindergarten painting sold for a staggering $75,000 in 2004, after a crazy bidding war erupted between parents. The colorful abstract of children and animals had been painted by a pre-school class at St. Catherine's School in Melbourne, Australia.

Love is in the Air

Japanese sweethearts Hirotomo Yoshikawa and Tomomi Sato were married in a Tokyo shopping center in 2003—while suspended by a wire 23 ft (7 m) above the ground. Relatives were able to watch the ceremony from a nearby staircase.

A Flying Start

A grandmother from Somerset, England, who had never flown before, took to the skies in 2004 to wing-walk while dressed as a witch. The plane carrying 72-year-old Mattie Williams, reached 100 mph (161 km/h).

The Name of the Game

In 2002, Richard James from St. Albans, England, agreed to change his name to Mr. Yellow-Rat Foxysquirrel Fairydiddle in exchange for a pint of beer. What began as a pub dare ended with Richard paying £38 ($76) to change his name officially. He informed his bank and received a credit card in his strange new name, but when the novelty began to wear off he didn't have enough money to change his name back. He wailed: "I just want to be called Richard again."

Chamber of Horrors

Visitors to an extreme Halloween attraction at Universal Studios in Orlando, Florida, in October 2003 were able to confront their fear of creepy creatures. The brave participants poked their heads into a cage containing scorpions, rats, cockroaches, worms, or snakes! Talk about facing your fears...

On Your Bike!

The World Mountain Bike Bog Snorkelling Championship is held near the town of Llanwrtyd Wells, where a water-filled trench is cut into a peat field. Riders plunge into the water on specially prepared mountain bikes weighed down with lead, and race along two lengths of the bog—approximately 100 yd (90 m)—without using any swimming strokes.

Guardian Angel

Jennifer Truman, of Lebanon, New Hampshire, was forced to land her parents' single-engine plane in 2004, despite having no flying experience. After her father passed out, Jennifer contacted an air traffic controller, who talked her safely to the ground.

Fright Wig

Things got hairy recently for passengers flying high on Coney Island's Cyclone roller coaster. A woman's wig flew off, jamming the ride's gears. During the 30 minutes it took for firefighters to untangle the hairpiece, the riders sat perched at the top of a 75-ft (23-m) drop.

Another Toe-nail in His Coffin

When British homeopathic healer Jack Temple died in 2004, as part of his estate

he left toenail clippings and hair strands of famous clients including Jerry Hall, Cherie Blair, and the late Princess Diana. The bizarre samples had been pickled in alcohol and stored at his clinic.

Way to Go!

Florida firm Eternal Ascent Society Inc. offer to send people's ashes into space in order to help families "let their loved ones go." The ashes go up in a biodegradable balloon which, at around 30,000 ft (9,000 m), freezes and then fractures, scattering the ashes into the wind. Their first customer was Star Trek fan Celeste Ready, of Ocala, Florida, who released her late mother's ashes in a yellow balloon at a park. She said her mother had always wanted to go into space.

Wrong Side of the Tracks

Gene Jackson, of New York, was able to walk along a single rail of a railroad track—on his hands!

333

Pigs Might Fly

When the Olympics went to Atlanta in 1996, the media said the Games were going to be run by a bunch of rednecks.

Some locals took mild offense at this and, led by D.J. Mac Davis, decided to stage their own Redneck Games in East Dublin, Georgia, to reinforce the stereotype. The games started in 1996 and have been held annually ever since. Events include typical redneck pastimes such as the mud pit belly flop, the hubcap hurl, a cigarette flip, a big hair contest and, the daddy of them all, the armpit serenade. Davis explains: "That's when you cup your hand under your armpit and make farting noises or tunes. In 1998, one contestant pumped out the entire theme tune to Green Acres!"

A hardy Redneck Games contestant holds his breath as he submerges his head under water, in a bid to bag a winning trotter.

A contestant comes up with a tasty trotter. Thank goodness no one thought of bobbing for pigs' feet at Halloween—apples are a whole lot sweeter!

Gebby Lehman strikes a perfect pose for the mud pit belly flop, while other competitors and spectators look on in awe as he dives into the pit of mud.

Paul Schneider chooses an alternative pose and jumps in the mud pit backwards!

Floating Home

Helicopter pilot Tim Graves and his family live on the ultimate mobile home. Their house near Ketchikan, Alaska, is a floating ex-logging camp that can be towed anywhere when not held by cables and anchor lines. It is accessible only by boat.

Fluffy Animals

Brazilian artist Tonico Lemos Auad fashions sculptures of squirrels, lions, and cats from bits of fluff that he scrapes off carpets.

Toenail Tapestry

In 2004, Uruguayan artist Carlos Capelan put on an exhibition of toenail clippings in Gateshead, England. He claimed that his work "playfully explores issues of self, ego, and identity."

Pen Friend

Collecting ball-point pens since childhood, Angelika Unverhau of Dinslaken, Germany, has gathered more than 220,000 of them from 146 countries.

Moose on the Loose

You might want to avoid Talkeetna, Alaska, during the town's annual "Moose Dropping Drop" contest, held the second weekend of July. For 32 years, these rowdies have been jumping into a hot-air balloon and dropping numbered pieces of moose dung on to a large "X" target. The winning flinger nabs $1,000 prize money.

Dirty Work

Ben Long, an English artist who draws in the dirt on vans, was shortlisted for a £10,000

Hitting the Nail on the Head

Francois Russell removes nails that have been hammered into a block of wood—with his teeth.

($20,000) art prize in 2002. Unless the vans are washed, his work can last for two months.

A Real Non-event

An antidote to other festivals, the Nothing Festival at Telluride, Colorado, promises no events whatsoever. The festival program simply announces: "Sunrises and sunsets as normal," and that "gravity will continue to be in effect." Visitors are duly thanked for kindly not participating.

Seeing Double

Geana Morris, of Glenolden, Pennsylvania, has beaten the odds: In August 2004, she gave birth to two sets of identical twins—two boys and two girls. Doctors say that the odds of doing so in a quadruplet birth is one in a million. Even more amazing is the fact that Geana is a twin herself, and she delivered the babies on her own birthday!

Hammering Home his Point

Leo Kongee, of Pittsburgh, Pennsylvania, known as "the Painless Wonder," could drive 60 penny nails into his nose, without experiencing any discomfort.

Running on Empty

Life's a gas for Mark Reiff. He has converted his suburban bungalow in Woodland, California, into an authentic, 1950s-style gas station!

Mark Reiff doesn't really sell fuel from his gas-station home, he just likes "to share fun with other people."

One of the pumps out front even offers gas at 11.4 cents per gallon—but don't bother lining up. For, like the other 25 antique pumps, it's just for show. Mark's imagination was fueled in 1999 when he bought an old gas pump at a yard sale to decorate his house. To emphasize that everything at Reiff's Gas Station is not as it seems, Mark has staged a mock car smash. There are suspicious skid marks on the road, a section of splintered fence, and the rear end of a classic 1956 Oldsmobile impaled in the side of a barn.

A 1956 Oldsmobile sticks out of the barn to give a clue that this is a gas station with a difference.

Believe It or Not!

You've Gotta Hand it to Her

This giant sculpture, titled "The Legend of Mother Earth", is made up of thousands of plants. It was one of 60 exhibits from 32 countries in an international exhibition of mosaiculture, or sculpting with plants, in downtown Montréal, Canada, in August 2003.

Sense of Identity

Scott Ginsberg, of St. Louis, Illinois, has worn a nametag every day since November 2, 2000, just to find out what would happen. He now works with people who want to become more approachable—and says wearing nametags is a great start.

Ship of Fools

For the Fools' Rules Regatta at Jamestown, Rhode Island, race contestants have two hours to build a sailable boat from non-marine items. One was even built from a Volkswagen car!

Washed Ashore

A very peculiar sight on South Bass Island in Lake Erie, Ohio, is that of an old boat that stands on dry land and is perched on the edge of a cliff. The 220-ton boat was rescued from scrap, and then converted into a family home. It was winched by crane to its present location.

Are You Lonesome Tonight?

If you don't have a special honey at home, don't fret: Entrepreneur James Wilson has launched "The Amazing Instant Mate" CD. A sultry male or female voice welcomes you home, asks about your day and tells you dinner is ready. The purpose of the CD, says Wilson, is emotional encouragement for those who are lonely.

Bulldozer Building

The office building of the United Equipment Company alongside freeway 99 in Turlock, California, was designed to look like a giant bulldozer. The boss has his office where the engine should be.

Grains of Truth

This impressive image of the Pope was one of the stunning sculptures made entirely from sand for the 2004 Sand Sculpture Festival on Blankenberge Beach in Belgium.

Inside Looking Out

A fully functioning bathroom was unveiled as a public piece of art in 2003. American artist Monica Bonvicini created a minimalist glass cube containing a usable lavatory. It was situated outside an art gallery in London, England.

Crazy Golf

Founded by a professional photographer, Douglas Keister, in 1988, Lucifer's Anvil golf course is located right in the heart of Nevada's inhospitable Black Rock Desert. The greens themselves are actually spray-painted on to the course—and they come in a variety of patterns, including a chessboard, a patch of freeway, and even a suburban living-room. Putts often reach 150 yd (140 m) and the players travel around the distance of the course on mountain bikes.

Eat Your Art Out

Jim Opasik, a sculptor from Baltimore, Maryland, creates intricate insects, animals, and human figurines from recycled cutlery and everyday kitchen utensils. Among his works of art are a coiled snake made out of overlapping spoons, a wolf spider made from prongs of forks, and an 8 ft (2.4 m) seahorse made of 82 cheese graters and 1,200 spoons, with serving platters for fins and strainers for the snout.

Night Moves

Artist Lyle Estill built a life-size chess set for night games in his backyard. He says that his only regret is he put it too close to the house: "Some nights when I was lying in bed, I could see torch light flickering on the ceiling because players had shown up for a game without me."

Outside Looking In

From the outside it may look like a stylish, mirrored public convenience, but once inside, it takes courage and nerve to use it!

Con-duct Unbecoming

Melody Williams of Greers Ferry, Arkansas, has a tacky hobby: Making shoes, clothes, jewelry, sculptures, and cards out of duct tape. She has even written a song about her love of it, ending: "may the gray never end."

Sleeping Booty

In April 2004, London's National Portrait Gallery showed an hour-long video of England soccer star David Beckham—sleeping! Artist Sam Taylor-Wood recognized that there was an abundance of action images of the sporting hero and she wanted to focus on a totally original feature of the much-photographed Beckham.

International Date Lines

At London's Nelson's Column in 2004, guest performers took turns reading Japanese artist On Kawara's book that consists solely of 271,000 selected dates between 998,031 BC and AD 1,001,980. The organizers claimed that the passage of

time, as depicted in the book, was extremely relevant to our everyday lives.

Homespun Brew

A German priest has started brewing beer in the most unusual place—his household washing machine. By building a computer interface into the washer so that it could run an automatic brewing program, Michael Fey, from Duisberg, Germany, is able to brew as much as 60 pt (30 l) of the beverage every six weeks.

Food, the Final Frontier

Entrepreneur Andy Gee is building a science-fiction themed restaurant he's calling "Starship Pegasus," 40 mi (64 km) outside Dallas, Texas. Modeled on the spacecraft from *Star Trek: The Next Generation*, the restaurant will feature space-themed dishes and game consoles that will allow diners to interact with players on the Internet. Gee has high hopes for a franchise chain.

Urban Space Men

Visitors to Italy could be forgiven for thinking that aliens have landed. Instead, it's simply a home with a twist—a private house in the shape of a spaceship. Take me to your kitchen...

Mystery Man

One night in 1971, D.B. Cooper vanished near Aerial, Washington, with $200,000 in ransom money after hijacking a jet. Since 1974 the town has held an annual D.B. Cooper party, to celebrate his claim to fame. As many as 500 fans gather to remember someone they never knew.

Stupid Parade

St. Stupid is the patron saint of the First Church of the Last Laugh, presided over by the Supreme Pontiff, Bishop Joey. Each April he leads the St. Stupid's Day Parade through the streets of San Francisco, California. The finale is a mass sock fight.

Chair-lift

Jackie Del Rio was able to lift two tables and six chairs using only his teeth—and as if that wasn't enough, he could also lift a chair with someone on it.

A Lot of Bottle

George Plumb used more than 200,000 bottles to recreate some famous landmarks on a 1-acre (0.4-ha) site in British Columbia, Canada. The retired carpenter began in 1962 with a five-room Bottle Castle, soon adding a Taj Mahal and a Leaning Tower of Pisa.

Gimme Shelter

Thanks to local schoolboy Bobby Macauley, passengers can wait in one of the world's most luxurious bus shelters—with lace curtains, a comfy sofa, plants, a hot-snacks counter, and a TV set! When the old shelter in the Shetland Islands, Scotland, was knocked down because of a leaking roof, Bobby, then seven years old, petitioned for a new one. Bobby maintains the shelter with a little help from his mom, who bakes the cakes, and a neighbor who waters the plants daily.

Artery Attack

When artist Shihan Hussaini displayed 56 portraits of Jayalalithaa, one of India's leading female politicians, in February 2004, it was an exhibition with a difference. For every portrait was painted in the artist's own blood, drawn from his body with medical assistance over a period of 20 days.

Risky Business

In April 2004, 32-year-old Ashley Revell liquidated all his worldly possessions to gamble the cash on just one single spin of the roulette wheel in Las Vegas, Nevada, as part of the reality TV series *Double or Nothing*. Fortunately for Ashley, Lady Luck was with him: He doubled his money when the ball settled on red number 7, winning him $270,600.

Feathered Friends

The hills are alive with the sound of quacking when the World Duck Calling Championships come to Stuttgart, Arkansas, every November. Each contestant must perform a hail call, a mating call, a feed call, and a comeback call within 90 seconds. The first national title was claimed back in 1936 by Thomas E. Walsh, one of only two competitors ever to win without the assistance of an artificial duck call. Instead, Walsh relied on creating the duck sounds in the back of his throat.

Top Bill

A staggering 10,000 rubber ducks compete in the annual Great Topeka Duck Race at Lake Shawnee, Kansas.

Hot Spot

The world's tallest thermometer doesn't contain a drop of mercury. It stands 134 ft (40 m) tall in a parking lot at Baker, California, its height marking the hottest-ever temperature in nearby Death Valley—134°F (57°C), back in 1913.

Ducks Run Amuck

A man paddles through a sea of plastic ducks during the annual Singapore Duck Race in 2001.

Quackers!

Charlotte Lee, of Los Angeles, California, owns more than 1,400 rubber ducks, including vintage ducks, red, pink, and blue ducks—and of course Donald and Daffy.

Baby Ducks

Topsy Turvy

A roller skater was suspended by the steel wheels of one skate attached to a magnet, made by the Dings Magnetic Separator Co. of Milwaukee.

Eat Your Heart Out

Russian Romeo Nikolay Kozlov announced that he was planning to sue his ex-girlfriend for the return of chocolates and other food he had given her. She told the court that she could not return the presents, such as Swiss chocolates, nuts, 6 lb (3 kg) of bananas, and "a bright red apple," because she had already eaten them!

Rat Race

Indian politician Jai Shankar unsuccessfully campaigned for the Indian national elections in 2004, by holding a live rat in his mouth to show support for starving farmers.

Where's the Beef?

Don Gorske, from Wisconsin, consumed his 20,000th Big Mac on July 19, 2004. The burger-gobbling feat took him 32 years—and he's been eating an average of two Big Macs every day since 1972.

Junk Art

Konstantin Simun, an artist from Boston, Masschusetts, works with one type of material—junk. He uses such items as old tires and traffic cones to create his works of art. He once made his own version of Michelangelo's "La Pieta" entirely from cut-up plastic bottles.

A Couple of Swells

Rich "The Locust" LeFevre and his wife Carlene are known as the "First Couple" of competitive eating. Carlene is ranked ninth in the world; Rich is ranked fifth. In July 2004, the Nevada couple were placed first and second in the "Swellin' with Melon" contest held in Ohio. Rich downed 11¼ lb (5 kg) of melon, while Carlene managed 9½ lb (4.3 kg).

To Be or Not To Be

The Woodstock Opera House, in Illinois, is thought to be haunted by the ghost of "Elvira," an actress said to have committed suicide in the theater. Elvira apparently likes seat number 113, and witnesses swear they have seen the seat lower mysteriously. A few even claim to have caught a glimpse of her long, pale hair.

Life on Mars

Hoping some day to walk on the red planet, members of the Mars Society volunteer for two-week stints in secluded habitats, which they hope might simulate the planet's conditions. Always keeping meticulous records, the members wear helmets made from plastic light fixtures and trash-can lids when heading outdoors. The society's 5,000 members, many of whom are NASA employees, are still on the lookout for "a few good Martians" to join them.

To Dial For

An Arkansas football fan was held for questioning even though he was completely unaware of what he had done. His cell phone, which was in his back pocket, had automatically called 911—not once but 35 times—as he jumped up and down while cheering, and the police eventually traced the calls and picked him up before he left the stadium.

California Dreaming

Architect Eugene Tsui has designed a home for his mother in Berkeley, California, that resembles a fish. The round house even has fin-like structures to dissipate rain.

Letting Rip

In 2004, Ed Charon, of Portland, Oregon, reclaimed his crown as the world's greatest ripper of telephone books. The 69-year-old managed to tear through a staggering 39 Portland white-page directories in just three minutes, beating the previous record of 30, which was held by Indiana fitness instructor Mike West.

Bra-vo!

In January 2001, San Francisco artist Emily Duffy asked friends and family to send her all their old bras. As contributions came in from across the globe, Emily patiently hooked the bras together, end to end, to form a round sculpture known as the "BraBall." By November 2003, the work was complete. It stood 5 ft (1.5 m) tall, weighed 1,800 lb (816 kg) and contained no fewer than 18,085 bras, thanks to such generous support.

Patriot Games

Most people have a car parked outside their house, but not a family in Outreau, northern France. Each morning, they open the curtains to be greeted by an enormous bust of former French president, François Mitterand, sculpted from metal and concrete, and covered with grass.

Out of his Tree

Belgian performance artist Benjamin Verdonck chose a weird stage on which to perform his new show in 2004. He was perched in a giant replica of a swallow's nest, 98 ft (30 m) above the ground, on the side of the Anspach Building in Brussels. From this precarious perch, he then tried to conduct conversations with passers-by on the street below.

This Art is Rubbish!

Leo Sewell transforms trash into treasure—and he can sell it for up to $50,000.

Ripley's

JUNK ART DONKEY

EXHIBIT NO: 10220

LEO SEWELL COLLECTED THE MATERIAL FOR THIS ART FROM PHILADELPHIA STREETS

Junk has a high price-tag once artist Leo Sewell gets his hands on it. He even makes sculptures of the deceased out of their own possessions.

All of Sewell's pieces are made from items that he finds in dumpsters and landfills. The Philadelphia-based artist uses old watches, plastic, medals, silverware, and clock parts to fashion life-size sculptures of animals and people.

Museums, corporations, and celebrities including Sylvester Stallone collect his work. People who feel strongly about recycling particularly admire his art. "I didn't set out to solve the world's problems with junk," says Sewell, "but I've gotten side benefits from the ecology movement." Lately, Sewell says he's been approached about creating realistic sculptures of people who have passed away, using their possessions.

RIPLEY's
JUNK ART MAN
EXHIBIT NO: 10219
CREATED BY LEO SEWELL, ENTIRELY OUT OF RECYCLED TOYS

Leo Sewell turns white elephants into priceless art.

That Really Takes the Biscuit

John Dobbins, of Glendora, New Jersey, lives in a three-story house that is shaped like a cookie jar!

It's a Steal

German artist Gerhard Zerbes announced that he did not want the public to buy pictures from his 2003 exhibition—he wanted people to steal them! Zerbes said the bizarre arrangement was intended to test human creativity and ingenuity in the face of surveillance cameras.

Feline Groovy

Humans take second place in the San Diego home of artists Frances Mooney and Bob Walker, because the house is designed as a luxury hotel for their cats. There is a cat gym, a 7 ft (2 m) scratching post, and 110 ft (33 m) of cat paths. Apart from the inevitable cat motifs, the décor is purple and pink—because cats apparently like those colors.

A Fridge Too Far

Ex-Royal Marine Paul McKelvey climbed the 3,560-ft (1,085-m) Mount Snowdon in 20 days—with a full-sized refrigerator strapped to his back. Beginning from his

home in Liverpool, England, Paul completed the 100-mi (161-km) charity trek to the summit of the Welsh mountain in four days. Although he removed the shelves and the motor, the refrigerator still weighed around 88 lb (40 kg). He said: "It started off as a joke, but then I decided to give it a go."

Wheels of Fortune

Sculptor Ptolemy Elrington, from Brighton, England, creates works of art from discarded auto hubcaps. He turns them into sharks, piranhas, and other fish and sells them for up to £1,500 ($1,800) each.

Snake Charmer

Liu Lang, China's infamous "snake man," has mastered some bizarre skills. He can lift a bucket of water using his eyeballs, swallow steel bearings and then spurt them from his mouth, eyes, nose, or ears, and lead a snake in through his nostril and out through his mouth.

Having a Whale of a Time

In the 1950s, Eero Saarinen designed Ingalls Hockey Rink at Yale University in New Haven, Connecticut, in the shape of a whale! The "dorsal fin" undulates into the roof and beneath its black "nose," the whale's "mouth" opens to welcome 3,000 spectators.

The Best Possible Taste

James Whistler, the famous American artist, once dyed his rice pudding green so that it didn't clash with the walls of his dining room!

Stretch Limbo

In 2003, Chilean artist Sebastian Mahaluf staged an exhibition consisting of an otherwise empty room, which he filled with more than 200 elastic bands stretched from wall to wall. Visitors were forced to turn themselves into contortionists in order to cross the room and reach the rest of Santiago's Balmaceda gallery.

Car Crazy

Auto-mad architect Dan Scully has built his New Hampshire home in the shape of a car. It has two round windows as headlights and even the bumper from a Volkswagen bus. The theme is continued inside, where old car seats provide the furniture and the bathroom tiles mimic tire tread!

Potty Pictures

Virginia Williams, who lives in Providence, Rhode Island, is captivated by photographs of toilets and has more than 100 in her collection.

Hat Tricks

The Red Hat Society, primarily for women over 50 who meet to celebrate middle age, has become a cultural phenomenon. It was founded just six years ago with 18 members, and there are now 33,000 chapters with 750,000 members across the U.S.A. These fun-loving gals are easily identified by their red hats, purple clothing, and huge smiles.

Fungi Fun

Visitors to Charlevoix, Michigan, could be forgiven for thinking that they have wandered into an enchanted forest. In the 1950s, Earl Young built an estate of homes with a difference—they all look like mushrooms.

Jump on the Bandwagon

The VW Bug that Harrod Blank calls "Pico De Gallo" is covered in records and working instruments. It is a tribute to rock 'n' roll. Harrod, an art car photographer, has created many more art cars.

On Top of the World

U.S. sailor Alvin "Shipwreck" Kelly spent more than 20,000 hours of his life sitting on top of flagpoles as part of a craze during the 1920s. He once sat for 49 consecutive days atop a pole in Atlantic City.

Shark Attack

Since 1986, the strangest house exterior in Britain has been a terraced home in Oxford owned by American Bill Heine. Heine's house has a 25-ft (7.6-m) fiberglass sculpture of a shark buried nose-down in the roof—a symbol, he claims, of man's inhumanity.

A Shining Example

Before his death in 2002, Dr. Hugh Hicks, a dentist from Baltimore, Maryland, collected more than 75,000 light bulbs from all around the world.

The Quiet Man

Jim Sulkers, of Manitoba, Canada, led such a reclusive life that when he died at home in 2002 at the early age of just 52, it was another two years before his mummified body was eventually discovered by the police. In all that time, not one of the neighbors had noticed that he wasn't around.

Pillow Talk

The folk of Kenwood, California, have a unique way to celebrate Independence Day—with the World Pillow Fighting Championships. Competitors, who straddle a slippery pole while holding a wet feather pillow, must knock their opponent off the pole using only the pillow. Kicking is forbidden and contestants must swing their pillow at least once every 30 seconds to avoid disqualification.

Homes from Home

Despite being more than 8,000 mi (12,870 km) from Germany, the town of Leavenworth, Washington State, was reborn in the 1960s as a Bavarian themed village. Authentic Bavarian shops sell wooden clocks and there is a Great Bavarian Ice Festival in January, conducted to the sound of alpine horns.

Bird Fancier

Linda Briggs, from Gloucestershire, England, has amassed more than 1,500 toy penguins. Her husband Tom also became part of the collection when he had images of penguins tattooed on his arms and chest.

Inflation Proof

Inflation holds no fears for Bilby Wallace, which is just as well because the former astronaut lives in an inflated house. The residence, situated in the Rockies and designed by architect Jonathan Zimmerman, is built around an inflated balloon. To help anchor the reinforced nylon walls, the rear of the house is 12 ft (4 m) underground.

Up, Up, and Away

Ever since seeing a movie in which a boy floated away on a string of balloons, Englishman Ian Ashpole had dreamed of emulating the feat. In 2001, the 46-year-old achieved his goal by filling 600 toy balloons with helium and sailing to a height of 11,000 ft (3,353 m) over the Cambridgeshire countryside. When the balloons started popping owing to the extreme altitude, he cut himself free with a knife and parachuted safely to the ground.

Steely Bite

To celebrate the Chinese New Year in Beijing, February 2007, this performer showed off his strength by taking a big bite out of a stainless steel saucepan lid.

Lights On, Nobody Home

In 2001, English artist Martin Creed won the prestigious Turner Prize and £20,000 ($39,000) for a piece of work entitled "The Lights Going On and Off"—which consisted simply of an empty gallery and a pair of flashing lights. His previous works have included crumpled balls of paper and sticky-tac sculptures.

Presidential Pets

After secretly collecting samples of fur from the Reagans' dog, Lucky, Claire McLean became so fascinated with the history of White House pets that she founded the Presidential Pet Museum in Lothian, Maryland. More than 1,500 items relate to such diverse creatures as Calvin Coolidge's racoons, an alligator presented to John Quincy Adams, and the Kennedy children's hamsters.

Nice to Meat You

Chilean artist Alejandra Prieto opened a new exhibition in 2004, in which all her works were made out of meat! One piece was a recreation of a scene from Little Red Riding Hood in which the wolf, whose ears were made from bacon, was hiding under bed covers made from ham.

Cave Dwelling

Fearing Armageddon, millionaire John Hay bought a plot of land near Parthenon, Arkansas, in the 1960s and developed a luxury bomb shelter in a cave. Now a private dwelling, it has a natural waterfall in the lounge.

It's in the Can

A scaled-down replica of St. Peter's Basilica was constructed in Rome from 10 million used aluminum cans.

A Real Tongue-lashing

In 1938, Leona Young, of New York, known as "the Devil's Daughter," used a regulation plumber's torch to pass flames over her tongue.

Wrap Artist

In 2003, British sculptor Antony Gormley wrapped 240 nude models in saran wrap and made plaster casts of their bodies. He had more than 1,000 volunteers ranging in age from five to 95.

Body Art

Two Chilean artists opened an exhibition of artwork in 2003—made from human body parts. Carmen Ariztia and Francisca Aninat's pieces included hairbrushes made out of hair and crosses made out of bones and teeth.

Taking the Plunge

Every New Year's Day, some 300 tuxedo-clad swimmers dive into the icy waters of Mackerel Cove, Rhode Island, for the Penguin Plunge.

FRONT COVER AND TITLE PAGE Reuters/Claro Cortes; 12 (t) Anuruddha Lokuhapuarachchi/Reuters, (c/t) Morten Nordby/Rex Features; 16 Sam Barcroft/Rex Features; 18 Rex Features; 19 Reuters; 21 SON/NAP/Rex Features; 22–23 Lewis Whyld/Rex Features; 24 United National Photographers/Rex Features; 26–27 Anuruddha Lokuhapuarachchi/Reuters; 29 Sipa Press/Rex Features; 31 Nils Jorgensen/Rex Features; 33 Anuruddha Lokuhapuarachchi/Reuters; 34–35 Morten Nordby/Rex Features; 36 Simon Kwong/Reuters; 37 Yuriko Nakao/Reuters; 38–39 David Gray/Reuters; 40 (t) Mike Poloway/Rex Features, (b) United National Photographers/Rex Features; 41 Darren Banks/Rex Features; 47 (t/l) Sipa Press/Rex Features, (r) HOM/Rex Features; 48 Sukree Sukplang/Reuters; 50–51 South West News Service/Rex Features; 52–53 Peter Brooker/Rex Features; 55 Jon Super/Rex Features; 56 (t) TDY/Rex Features, (c/t) Romeo Ranoco/Reuters, (b) Northscot Press Agency/Rex Features; 63 (t) Ray Tang/Rex Features; 64 Nils Jorgensen/Rex Features; 65 Northscot Press Agency/Rex Features; 66–67 Greg Williams/Rex Features; 67 (t) Charles M. Ommanney/Rex Features; 71 David Bebber/Reuters; 72 David Grey/Reuters; 74 Action Press/Rex Features; 75 TDY/Rex Features; 78 Romeo Ranoco/Reuters; 85 Nils Jorgensen/Rex Features; 86–87 Stringer/Reuters; 88–89 SWS/Rex Features; 91 HO/Reuters; 92–93 Phil Yeomans/Rex Features; 94 Rex Features; 95 Mike Blake/Reuters; 96 Patrick Barth/Rex Features; 97 Rex Features; 99 David Hartley/Rex Features; 100 (c/t) SCANPIX/Reuters, (b) Action Press/Rex Features; 104–105 Marcos Brindicci/Reuters; 106 Action Press/Rex Features; 108 Alessia Pierdomenico/Reuters; 109 Masatoshi Okauchi/Reuters; 111 Desmond Boylan/Reuters; 112–113 Sam Barcroft/Rex Features; 114–115 Erika Nelson/World's Largest Things/www.WorldsLargestThings.com; 117 David Loh/Reuters; 118–119 Romeo Ranoco/Reuters; 118 (t) Chip East/Reuters; 120 "Wonders of Science", Whittier, CA, USA; 121 "Red Boots Productions", Hollywood, CA, USA; 122 Andrea/Rex Features; 123 Stringer/Reuters; 124–125 Reuters; 127 Adrian Sherratt/Rex Features; 128–129 Paul Gillis/Rex Features; 129 (t) HO/Reuters (b) South West News Service/Rex Features; 130–131 Dan Riedlhuber/Reuters; 132–133 George A. Blair; 134–135 SCANPIX/Reuters; 136 Howard Walker/Rex Features; 138 John Powell/Rex Features; 139 Phil Yeomans/Rex Features; 140–141 © Amy C. Elliot; 142 Action Press/Rex Features; 143 Andrew Winning/Reuters; 144 (t) Mike Walker/Rex Features, (c/b) Andy Newman/AFP/Getty Images, (b) Issei Kato/Reuters; 148–149 Mike Walker/Rex Features; 150 Leon Schadeberg/Rex Features; 151 Masatoshi Okauchi/Reuters; 152–153 Issei Kato/Reuters; 158–159 Alex Grimm/Reuters; 158 (b) Kimimasa Mayama/Reuters; 160–161 Paul Cooper/Rex Features; 162–163 Reuters; 164 Mark Campbell/Rex Features; 166–167 Andy Newman/AFP/Getty Images; 168 John Chapple/Rex Features; 169 AFP/Getty Images; 170 Paul Jones/AFP/Getty Images; 171 Simon Baker/Reuters; 173 Getty Images; 174–175 Paul Cooper/Rex Features; 175 EDPPics/Usher/Rex Features; 177–178 Rex Features; 179 Phil Yeomans/Rex Features; 181 Alisdair Macdonald/Rex Features; 182 Dan Riedlhuber/Reuters; 183 (t) Tim Wimborne/Reuters, (b) Rex Features; 184 Paul Nicholls/Rex Features; 186–187 Sukree Sukplang/Reuters; 188 (t) Fatih Saribas/Reuters, (c/t) Mark Campbell/Rex Features, (c/b) PB/Rex Features, (b) Toby Melville/Reuters; 192 Mark Campbell/Rex Features; 193 Lewis Durham/Rex Features; 194 Rob Howarth/Rex Features; 195 Fatih Saribas/Reuters; 196–197 Rex Features; 197 (r) PB/Rex Features; 199 Erik C Pendzich/Rex Features; 201 Daniela Larini/Rex Features; 202–203 Edgar Mullar/Manfred Stader/Rex Features; 204 Sam Tinson/Rex Features; 210–211 Toby Melville/Reuters; 210 (t) Stringer/Reuters; 212 Claro Cortes/Reuters; 218 Reuters; 219 Peter Brooker/Rex Features; 221 B Mathur/Reuters; 222–223 Karl Schoendorfer/Rex Features; 224 Kamal Kishore/Reuters; 225 Reuters; 227 Tobias Schwarz/Reuters; 231 Ponopresse/Rex Features; 232 (t) EDPPics/Usher/Rex Features, (c/b) Ray Tang/Rex Features, (b) Rex Features; 237 Henry Romero/Reuters; 239 Adrian Sherratt/Rex Features; 242 Mimmo Frassineti/Rex Features; 243 Paul Cooper/Rex Features; 244 Tony Larkin/Rex Features; 245 (t/l) Tony Larkin/Rex Features, (t/r) EDPPics/Usher/Rex Features (b) A Rodriguez/Rex Features; 246 Toshifumi Kitamura/AFP/Getty Images; 247 Assignments Photographers/Rex Features; 248–249 24/7 Media/Rex Features; 251 Mike Walker/Rex Features; 252–253 Nigel Tisdall/Rex Features; 254 NWI/Rex Features; 257 SWS/Rex Features; 260 Assignments Photographers/Rex Features; 262–263 HO/Reuters; 262 (t) Sipa Press/Rex Features; 266–267 Gerry Penny/AFP/Getty Images; 266 (b) Nils Jorgensen/Rex Features; 267 Nils Jorgensen/Rex Features; 268–269 Ray Tang/Rex Features; 270–271 Norm Betts/Rex Features; 272 Rowan Griffiths/Rex Features; 273 Reuters; 274 Rex Features; 276 (c/t) John Gurzinski /AFP/Getty Images, (c/b) Eric C. Pendzich/Rex Features, (b) Getty Images; 278–279 Eric C. Pendzich/Rex Features; 280 Nils Jorgensen/Rex Features; 281 Ralph Merlino/Rex Features; 282 Mike Carmichael; 284–285 Drew Gardner/Rex Features; 286 Tim Shaffer/Reuters; 287 ZZ/XXD/SPL/Rex Features; 290 Lee Besford/Reuters; 291 Boston Herald/Rex Features; 292 Dan Charity/ Rex Features; 293 JZB/Rex Features; 294–295 John Gurzinski /AFP/Getty Images; 296 Nils Jorgensen/Rex Features; 299 Shannon Stapleton/Reuters; 301 Getty Images; 303 Alban Donohoe/Rex Features; 304 Lindsey Parnaby/Rex Features; 305 ACM/UTN/ZZ/Rex Features; 306 Simon Jones/Rex Features; 307 Stringer/India/Reuters; 308–309 Geoff Wilkinson/Rex Features; 310–311 Brendan Beirne/Rex Features; 311 (c) SWS/Rex Features; 312 Jagadeesh NV/Reuters; 314 Doug Hall/Rex Features; 315 Peter Brooker/Rex Features; 316 Nils Jorgensen/Rex Features; 317 Sukree Sukplang/Reuters; 319 Ali Jarekji/Reuters; 320 (c/b) Luis Enrique Ascui/Reuters, (b) Peter Brooker/Rex Features; 324–325 Peter Macdiarmid/Reuters; 327 Brian Harris/Rex Features; 328–329 Colin Shepherd/Rex Features; 330–331 Universal Orlando/Kevin Kolczynski/Reuters; 332 Huw Evans/Rex Features; 334 (t) Dan Callister/Rex Features, (b) Reuters/Tami Chappell; 335 Reuters/Tami Chappell; 338–339 Stewart Cook/Rex Features; 340 Shaun Best/Reuters; 341 Denis Closon/Rex Features; 344–345 Sipa Press/Rex Features; 347 (t) Nick Young Bateman/Rex Features, (b) Features North/Rex Features; 348–349 Peter Brooker/Rex Features; 348 (b/r) Luis Enrique Ascui/Reuters; 352 Lefevre Sylvain/Sipa/Rex Features; 353 Francois Lenoir/Reuters; 356–357 STR/Reuters; 358–359 Peter Brooker/Rex Features; 361 Reuters/Claro Cortes; 362 Reuters.

All other photos are from MKP Archives and Ripley's Entertainment Inc.
Every attempt has been made to acknowledge correctly and contact copyright holders and we apologize in advance for any unintentional errors or omissions, which will be corrected in future editions.